NAI NAI
STORY TIME

**A legacy of the struggles and opportunities
of a Chinese immigrant, imbued with
Grandma's wisdom and humor**

ANLY KANG HSU

ISBN: 979-8-89694-437-9 - Ebook
ISBN: 979-8-89694-438-6 - Paperback
ISBN: 979-8-89694-439-3 - Hardcover

To Penny and Jeffrey, my pillars of support

To Henry, my wise monkey

To Samantha and Thomas, my joy and inspiration

CONTENTS

Introduction 9

Chapter 1: Sandy.. 17

Chapter 2: The New Immigrants...................................... 26

Chapter 3: My Father 49

Chapter 4: My Grandparents 57

Chapter 5: Atlantic City 68

Chapter 6: The Egg.. 80

Chapter 7: Teacher 88

Chapter 8: I Can't Do It.. 101

Chapter 9: Snow Storm 107

Chapter 10: Food for the Festivals 122

Chapter 11: Best Turkey.. 132

Chapter 12: Christmas Friend.. 138

Chapter 13: Heaven Awaits.. 143

Chapter 14: Mama Went Home.. 155

Chapter 15: Monkey Business.. 167

Chapter 16: The Misunderstood...................................... 176

References 195

ACKNOWLEDGEMENTS

It is with my deepest and most sincere gratitude that I thank my family, Penny, Jeffrey, and Shirley, whose perpetual compassion and undying understanding sustained me throughout my writing journey.

The courage and perseverance of my father and mother helped me revere and appreciate their sacrifices throughout the hardship and agony that plagued their lives.

This book is made possible with stories contributed by my siblings and friends who suffered during the Cultural Revolution. A special thank you to my sister, Jenrang, the tiny dragon lady, whose illness and fever paved the way for us to come to America.

Without the patience, and intelligence of Penelope and the computer expertise of Jeffrey, this book could never be completed. Thanks to Shirley Hsu and David Lott for their tireless efforts in helping me to clearly convey my thoughts and recollections throughout these stories.

INTRODUCTION

This collection of short stories is based on events from my life that happened in China and in America. The support and encouragement from my friends and relatives enabled me to put into words the adventures and misadventures that occurred.

As I approach three-quarter of centrury in life, I realize each new dawn is a gift on borrowed time and there is much to do before twilight finally sets upon me. Many unusual and incredible experiences, traumas, and dramas have affected my way of life and have made me the way I am. I want to pass down to my children and grandchildren a legacy of strength, perseverance, and tolerance. They need to know why I am wise and kind, foolish and quirky, all at the same time.

As an immigrant who survived a death-defying encounter on my journey to the US, I can sympathize with the plight of many current asylum-seeking migrants. Working hard since age twelve, I have worn many hats and cared for many people. These experiences have made me appreciate the complexity of the world and the determination of the strong and the brave who try to overcome adversity, right the wrong, and make a better world for us all.

It is also my intention with this book to enable my grandchildren and other Chinese descendants to be acquainted with at least some of the more important parts of our culture and history. May we never forget our ancestry and our quaint and complicated traditions. It is our imperfections that inspire us to improve. Our struggles strengthen our resolve to make our life better and brighter.

The events mentioned in this memoir are true, although many of these historical incidents have been deleted from the history books or sanitized by the Communist and the Nationalist governments. For this reason, many younger Chinese people and Chinese-Americans do not have much knowledge about the trials and tribulations millions of people in China struggled with throughout the years. Many children now living in both Communist and Republic of China are not aware of some of these events.

Although the stories I wrote are not in chronological order, a quick glimpse of Chinese history may add background and clarity that may help enlighten its importance and its effects on my family.

My family's arrival in America started with my maternal grandfather, who was only able to come to the US after the Chinese Exclusion Act of 1882 was revised to allow a very limited quota of Chinese people to immigrate to the US in 1924. His journey to America was facilitated by the Boxer Rebellion Indemnity Scholarship established in 1908. He was accepted by the University of Illinois and came to the US as a student in 1926. My maternal grandmother, on the other hand, was only able to come to the US in 1949 after the Chinese Exclusion Act was repealed in 1943. These restrictions enacted by the US government forced my grandparents to live on separate continents for twenty years.

In trying to flee Communist China, many Chinese people endured the difficult journey, first to Macau, a Portuguese colony ceded by China in 1887, then being smuggled to Hong

Kong which was ceded to Britain in 1842. As a British colony, Hong Kong provided better living conditions and a much-needed stepping stone to allow people to immigrate to other parts of the world.

My father, who stayed in China after the communists took over the country, was dehumanized and humiliated after my Mama took my sister Tina and me and left Shanghai to go to Hong Kong in 1959. The Communist government only allowed my mother to take my sickly sister and me to leave to get medical help. Sadly, the Red Guards tortured and paralyzed my father during the Cultural Revolution which started in 1966 and ended in 1976. He died of a massive stroke in 1974.

My brother Kyle and sister Jade, who also remained in China with my father, were sent to far away poor farms to be "re-educated" during the Cultural Revolution. My brother was not allowed to attend college. They were only able to come to New York after President Nixon visited China in 1972 and established a diplomatic relationship with China in 1979.

This book is a collection of events that happened to my family, starting with my maternal grandfather, who was born in 1899 in Qingtian, China, and ending with lessons for my eight-year-old granddaughter, Sandy. I hope she will learn more about our Chinese culture and traditions and how best to survive adversity and appreciate diversity. It's a story that expands five generations, integrating the eastern and western lifestyles. Hopefully, some of these stories will pique the interest for more discovery and appreciation of Chinese history and heritage.

Approximate and Abridged Timeline of Modern
Chinese History With Supplemental Information

Year	Significance	Comment
1840-1842	1st Opium War	Nanjing Treaty: China lost the war and had to pay indemnities. It ceded Hong Kong to Britain.
1856-1860	2nd Opium War	China lost again. Britain forced China to open more ports for trade and legalized the import of opium in China.
5/6/1882	US passes The Chinese Exclusion Act	Chinese were not allowed to immigrate to the US for forty years. The Exclusion Act was revised with severe restrictive quotas in 1924. It was finally repealed in 1943.
8/1894 to 4/1895	First Sino-Japanese War	Fought between China and Japan over control of Korea. China lost the war and ceded Taiwan and three provinces in Manchuria to Japan.
11/2/1899 to 9/7/1901	The Boxer Rebellion	The Yihetuan (Righteous and Harmonious Fists 義和團) was encouraged by Empress Dowager Cixi to push eight foreign countries out of China: Britain, Italy, Russia, Germany, France, America, Austria-Hungary and Japan. China lost the battle and had to pay $330 million in reparations to the eight countries who sent in approximately 20,000 troops combined. The US received $24 million for sending 200 marines to fight 55 days in Beijing. In 1909, the US realized that they were overpaid by the Chinese due to an error in the calculation of the exchange rate. It returned $11 million to China and established the Boxer Rebellion Indemnity Scholarship Program to help the elite Chinese scholars come to the US for a better education. With this scholarship, China was able to establish the prestigious Tsinghua College in Beijing in 1911. China Institute was established in NYC in 1926.
1911	Republic Of China established	With the fall of the Qing Dynasty, Sun Yat-sen tried to unite China as the Republic of China. His three principles: Nationalism, Democracy and Economic Socialism were inspired by Marxism, Leninism, and the Russian Revolution. Yuan Shikai was made the first president of the Republic of China due to his command of the military.

1912-1928	Warlord Years	There was an uprising of warlords after the fall of the Qing Dynasty. Warlords were either bandits, outlaws, or soldiers throughout China. Each wanted to be the king of their province with their own militia. Chiang Kai-shek purged and destroyed all of the warlords, leaving only the Nationalist and the Communist Parties in China. In 1924, Sun Yat-sen founded The Whampoa Military Academy in Guangzhou. Chiang Kai-shek was the principal. Russia sent military advisors to train the Chinese officers, both Nationalists and future Communists. The first four generations of officers later transformed China into either The Nationalist or the Chinese Communist Parties.
6/28/1919	Versailles Treaty	Japan declared war on Germany during WWI in support of Britain. When Germany was forced to concede its colonies to the Allied Forces, Britain, France and the United States decided to transfer German interests in Shandong, China to Japan. Both Germany and China were not allowed to negotiate. Thousands of Chinese students protested on 5/4/19. China did not sign the treaty. In 1922, Japan returned Shandong and all the German railways back to China for an unknown amount of compensation.
9/18/1931	Mukden Incident	Japan attacked Shenyang in Manchuria. Thousands of Chinese people escaped northern China to central and southern parts of China for safety. In 1932, Japan established a puppet state, Manchukuo, in Manchuria. The last Qing emperor, Puyi, was a puppet figurehead.
1927-1936	Chinese Civil War	Nationalist vs. Communist Simultaneous to the Japanese occupation of Manchuria, the nationalists and communists began a civil war for control of the rest of the country. Chiang Kai-shek wanted to kill Mao Zedong and neutralize the communists first, then deal with the Japanese. His Nationalist army pushed the communists out of Southeast China during the Long March.

10/1934-10/1935	Long March	The Chinese Communist Party left southeast China and marched toward northeast China to escape the Nationalists. They started with approximately 89,000 troops and crossed over 6,000 miles (10,000 kilometers) of mountains and rivers to reach Yan'an in Shaanxi province. They arrived with less than ten percent of their troops. Yan'an was mountainous and had very rugged terrain which made it difficult for the Nationalists to traverse and advance an attack. The Chinese Communist Party found a safe harbor in Yan'an and remained there until the end of World War II. It was estimated that 20 million Chinese and 10 million Japanese were killed during World War II.
Dec. 1936	Warlord Zhang Xueliang	Warlord Zhang Xueliang was pro-Nationalist but he was totally against killing Chinese people, including the communist Chinese troops which had increased to 30,000 soldiers. Zhang arrested Chiang Kai-shek in December 1936 in Xi'an, China. Zhang Xueliang wanted Chiang Kai-shek to work with the Chinese Communist Party to fight the Japanese. Chiang Kai-shek was released when he agreed to work with the Chinese Communist Party. He then placed Zhang under house arrest until 1960. However, the Communists stayed safely in Yan'an and did not participate in the second Sino-Japanese War, which became a part of World War II.
7/7/1937	Marco Polo Bridge Incident outside of Beijing	The Japanese traveled from Manchuria and created an incident on the Marco Polo Bridge outside of Beijing. This is the beginning of the second Sino-Japanese War, which was fought between Japan and the Nationalist Chinese army. The Japanese occupied Beijing, Tianjin, Nanjing, and then Shanghai.
Dec. 1937-Jan. 1938	Nanjing Massacre	The Japanese invaded Nanjing and killed an estimated 300,000 Chinese in six weeks.

1937-1945	Second Sino-Japanese War	The Second Sino-Japanese War was part of World War II. The Chinese military was supported by Russia and America with weapons to fight the Japanese. The Nationalist Army was the only Chinese soldiers battling the Japanese. The Second Sino-Japanese War weakened the Nationalists and gave the Communists the chance to thrive under the radar. The American Volunteer Group (AVG), known as the Flying Tigers was created by General Claire Chennault, who was hired by General Chiang Kai-shek as an aviation advisor. The Flying Tigers were paid by the Republic of China to patrol and protect the supply route from Burma, (Myanmar) to Kunming, China.
1945-1949	Chinese Civil War	Nationalists vs. Communists After the 2nd world war ended and Japan was ousted from China for the final time, the civil war between the Communists and Nationalists restarted. The Communists now had the support of Russia and all the weapons and planes left by the Japanese from WWII. Meanwhile, The US did not completely support the Republic of China because of the relentless corruption and instability of the Nationalist Party. Four countries, Russia, Britain, France, and the United States tried to broker a peaceful union between the two parties. Mao Zedong originally demanded eight conditions, and Chiang Kai-shek refused. Chiang's right-hand man, General Li Zongren, continued the peace talks and accepted the conditions. As the Nationalists withdrew from Beijing, the Communists continued to fight on. Mao Zedong increased his demand to twenty-four conditions, including the punishment of the four very elite and wealthy Chinese political families, Chiang, Soong, Kung, and Chen. General Li refused. The communists proceeded to occupy Beijing and Nanjing. The Nationalist party collapsed.
1949	People's Republic of China was formed	The Nationalist party fled to Taiwan between April and December in 1949. They took gold and silver from China and treasures from the National Palace Museum. Chiang used the gold to establish the political and economic systems of the Republic of China in Taiwan. Mao established the People's Republic of China on 10/1/49.

1959-1962	Great Leap Forward	Great Leap Forward was a plan put into motion by the Communist Party that encouraged uneducated farmers to continually yield better and higher crop production numbers. Out of fear of being punished harshly for not making these quotas, farmers began reporting numbers that were unrealistic. Unable to meet the quotas, farmers ate nothing but tree bark, sending every grain of food they had to the government. Millions of Chinese died from starvation.
1966-1976	Cultural Revolution	The Chinese Communist Party arrested, beat, and killed anyone who they deemed as being a member of the Five Black Categories: Wealthy Farmers, Landlords, Counter-revolutionaries, Right-wingers, and Bad Influencers. These people were humiliated in public, beaten by the Red Guards, and forced to make posters for all to see professing their supposedly shameful lifestyles and beliefs. The Red Guards destroyed any symbols of Confucianism, feudal cultures, Buddhism, Christianity and old traditions like Peking Opera. It was estimated that millions of Chinese were killed. Hundreds of thousands of Chinese people committed suicide; many were teachers and intellectuals. The schools and theaters for Peking Opera were all destroyed. The actors were humiliated or killed. Tsinghua College was damaged severly in 1966. Schools were shut down so that the young students could join the Red Guards to cleanse China of the "Black Five Categories."
Feb.1972	Nixon's Visit	Nixon visited China. The US recognized the People's Republic of China, granting the communist country official status.
9/27/1972	Tanaka's Visit	Mao Zedong thanked the Japanese Prime Minister Kakuei Tanaka for invading China in World War II. Mao did not demand any reparations from Japan for killing 20 million Chinese people
Dec.1978		China opened trade with the West.
6/4/1989	Tiananmen Square Massacre	No confirmed data on how many Chinese college students, supporters, and advocates for democracy were killed by hundreds of military tanks crushing the protestors when the lights went out on that bloody night.
7/1/1997	Hong Kong returned to China	Britain ended 158 years of governance and returned Hong Kong to China.
10/24/ 2018	Hong Kong - Zhuhai - Macau Bridge	The 55-kilometer-long bridge and tunnel system connected Macau to Hong Kong.

CHAPTER 1

SANDY

In October 2016, fifty plus years after we arrived on American soil, I was sitting in the office of a neonatal surgeon at Long Island Jewish Hospital with both hands clasped together, saying a silent prayer for my daughter-in-law, Grace. Her obstetrician had referred her here because her fetus, my first grandchild, was two weeks behind on her growth. Bi-weekly sonograms and fetal monitoring were promptly scheduled. Everyone was worried that the baby would be born prematurely with physical or mental developmental issues.

After five weeks of regular monitoring, the baby reached the earliest date for safe delivery via induced labor. The brain and the lungs were ready to take on the challenges of the real world at thirty-four weeks and one day.

Waiting was torturous. All sorts of "what if" scenarios were imagined. What if she was born blind or mute? What if she was missing limbs? What if she had a defective heart, or lungs, or brain? Unlike the old days when family members paced back and forth frantically outside the delivery room, the new waiting room environment was very quiet. Everyone was sitting, keeping busy texting. I was puzzled and questioned how they could even concentrate to type on a two-inch keyboard with two big thumbs.

After ten hours, baby Sandy was delivered via cesarean section. She announced her arrival with high-pitched wailing and screaming. She was a tiny, perfectly normal, three-pound, thirteen-ounce diva singing an operatic aria: "See me! Feed me! Feed me! Now! Now!"

Bravo!

My mama was so happy to hear that her first great-granddaughter, Sandy, was healthy and that the medical technology and equipment was so sophisticated now. My sister, Tina, was born in 1953, also prematurely, weighing two pounds. Everyone said Tina would never survive. Some even suggested that the hospital should end her tiny life to prevent her suffering in the future. Thank God, my mama did not give up. Tiny Tina eventually became the main reason why my whole family moved to America.

Sandy was in the NICU, or Neonatal Intensive Care Unit, for four days. The benchmark for infant discharge was no longer weight related. Instead, if the baby was able to sit or sleep with its head held up in a car seat for one and a half hours, then it could be cleared to go home. Sandy, the precious first granddaughter for me, came home when she weighed only three pounds, ten ounces, which was seven times smaller than an average turkey served at Thanksgiving.

Like most babies, Sandy drooled and pooped all the time. Hiccups and spit-ups kept everyone busy. She was satiated after each feeding and looked intoxicated most of the time. She had many easy and lazy days. She gained one ounce each day, and by the ripe old age of 45 days, she had doubled her birth weight to seven pounds, ten ounces.

Quickly, she developed all the characteristics of a pampered aristocrat. She had chubby cheeks and a double chin. She demanded attention and immediate service with no regard to the time of day or night. Her ferocious appetite and overindulgence at Grace's milk buffet had caused her to develop a gastrointestinal disorder from a very rich diet—*gas*. She passed gas loudly and indiscriminately. Then she smiled, as the discomfort dissipated; gone with the wind went all of her troubles. Off she went again to dream in peace.

As a proud grandmother, I wanted the privilege of spoiling Sandy and left the disciplining to her parents. I wanted to buy all the toys for all her birthdays and special events, but, sadly, Toys-R-Us went bankrupt! How could that be possible? Where could I go to buy the fun toys (and educational ones too)? Learning to shop online was new to me. My son, Justin, had to teach me how to "surf the net."

Desktop computers or PCs were becoming obsolete. Most people were working with a laptop and a "*mouse.*" I had to relearn to type on a smaller surface. Point and click took some getting used to because I had dyslexia and very poor hand-eye coordination. I had no idea that every store can be found with the title, *name.com*. I was really impressed and pleasantly surprised by the search function. I was able to type in the name of what I remembered to be a toy, and lo and behold, dozens of toys with that name or description would pop up. It was great not traveling to the store and carrying packages home. Oh, my God, I love shopping at stores that offer *free delivery*.

I found it shocking that so much had changed since I had children. Disposable diapers were cheaper and more sanitary than the old-fashioned cloth diaper service we had used. The diapers now even had a strip to tell you when they were wet. Sandy had a protective head guard to keep the shape of her head round while sleeping, which was a complete novelty to me. If the baby had difficulty sleeping, specialists called doulas or baby sleep consultants were available to help. Wow. I really could have used their expertise when my daughter, Phoebe, was born. She cried every two hours until she was two years old.

A temperature-controlled merino wool blanket for sleep was unheard of when my kids, now adults, were young. Breast milk could be pumped by a small portable machine and stored in the freezer—that would've been a lifesaver for me. When I was breastfeeding Phoebe in the old days, she could only get milk from one breast. The other breast would leak while nursing, so the baby was never full, always crying every two hours for more milk.

My husband and my son bought a two-family house in Bayside, New York. Justin, Grace and Sandy lived upstairs with three bedrooms. My husband, William and I lived downstairs with two bedrooms. This living arrangement made it very easy to help care for Sandy.

Sandy was fortunate to have a large bedroom. In her palatial room, there was a bassinet, a crib, a playpen, a swing, a changing table, and two chests of drawers. I was told by Mama that I slept in a drawer for the first few months of my life, and my sister, Tina, slept in an armchair until she was able to sit up by herself. What a luxury little Sandy had, using her drawers for clothes!

At six months of age, Sandy liked to put everything in her mouth, especially her fingers and toes; she sucked them constantly. She could turn over and even tried to sit up. She could see colors and started to remember faces. Once she began to crawl, her small world began to open up to everything life has to offer. We rearranged the room to give her extra space for *exploration*. After all, she was "Queen of the Road," "Master of the House," and definitely the "Crowned Princess" who sat majestically on her throne, a semicircular pillow called Boppy.

Two summers later, Sandy was walking and talking like a general with little patience. Her verbal commands were very few, but clear. With her puckered lips, furrowed brows, and piercing big eyes, she would point to my hand and shout, "No! No! No!" She looked at my hand holding a banana and reached for it, saying, "Mine, mine, mine!" I immediately surrendered the banana and watched Sandy take a big bite and consume half of it.

Those two commands were repeated throughout the day. What was mine became Sandy's, along with her own treasure trove of dolls and toys. Sandy had no qualms about taking some of my possessions, like scarf, wallet, keys, and lipsticks, which she loved. It was shocking to me to discover that my two-year-old granddaughter was becoming a dictator, although a most adorable one.

Many daily activities occupied Sandy's hours. She would play with her kitchen toys, express her creative mind on her drawing pad, read a little, and help me repair the broken toys and stuffed animals that were damaged by you know who.

As the Generalissimo, her wish was my command. I tried to follow her orders and adjust to her ever-changing desires. But if my performance was not acceptable to the high standards of General Sandy, she would shout, "Top it, top it, top it!" Aha, the almighty Commander could not pronounce her S's. B's and L's were difficult for her as well. She was so adorable and melted my heart when she tried to say, "I wove you" and "Happy Dirt Day to you."

When I became exhausted and needed to rest, I would hold up a soft pink velour bunny and wave it like a white flag, surrendering. Sandy would dash into my arms to grab and rescue her precious bunny and would hold it up to her angelic face and relax comfortably in my lap while sucking her tiny thumb.

After hours of playing, running, and jumping, her royal highness finally needed a nap. I held this tiny, gentle body in my arms, rocking her tenderly as I whispered softly in her ear, "You are my priceless princess. You are mine, mine, mine."

At the ripe age of three years old, Sandy had grown to be an irresistible and beautiful munchkin. Babysitting a three-year-old child was not an easy, sedentary job. It required much energy, quick thinking, and inexhaustible physical agility.

On one such round of babysitting, Sandy greeted me joyously. She called me "Nai Nai," and immediately took me to her own little "store." She had set up a cash register next to her food items near the fireplace. She handed me a purse containing wooden coins and paper money from a Monopoly game.

"How much is the pizza?" I asked.

She looked at her pictorial price list and said, "Five dollars" while holding up two fingers. Instead of giving me a slice of pizza, she quickly changed her focus to the plastic flowers that she assembled in her make-believe garden and presented me with a purple flower which had a yellow pistil. She used her miniature watering can and pretended to water the flower.

Then, she took all the flower parts away and put them back in a colorful box. She closed the lid and handed me the box. "Surprise for you, Nai Nai. Open it." I graciously accepted the gift and gently opened the box which was much worn from being opened and closed multiple times. We smiled at each other as I took out one flower piece at a time. Sandy placed them next to each other in a straight line and said, "choo-choo train." Okay, another game just started.

I took out a wipe-clean activity book and erasable markers. Sandy tried to draw a line between two similar shapes. When the page was done, she erased the lines she made so that the page was all clean again. After a few moments, Sandy gave me the marker and commanded, "You do it. I am busy."

"What? What are you busy doing?"

"I am busy holding Bunny Boo," Sandy answered in a matter-of-fact voice, as she brought close to her face her once-pink-now-gray little velour bunny which has lost half an ear. Her delicate right thumb went into her tiny mouth, and she started to gently stroke her gray bunny with her dainty left hand.

Her favorite toys were dinosaurs. She could name ten different kinds of dinosaurs. I could not even pronounce most of their names. Sandy could say that the one with big teeth was the Tyrannosaurus, the one with spikes on its back was called Stegosaurus. Brachiosaurus was the one with the long neck and the flying one was the Pterodactyl. Of course, the one with three horns was called Triceratops. How could she pronounce these names? She was only three years old. I was especially thrilled on Christmas that year when Sandy gifted me a T-shirt printed with a T-Rex named Nai Nai-Saurus.

She loved to read rhyming books and tongue twisters. After a few readings of Dr. Seuss's *Fox in the Socks* and *Cat in the Hat*, she was ready to doze off. Nap time was always the best time of the day for me. My aching body was crying out for a little R&R—that meant rest and more rest. The darling little one crawled into my arm, hugging her Bunny Boo and sucking her thumb. I cuddled with her and sang a favorite Chinese lullaby to the sleepyhead.

The red sun has set behind the hill.
Little lambs want to go home.
The lambs are returning home.
Are all of your tummies full?
E Ya Hay. E Ya Hay.

The sky is dark, and the stars are bright.
Little lambs are following Mom.
Have no fear. Do not fear.
Mom has turned on the light.
E Ya Hay. E Ya Hay.

Sandy closed her eyes and relaxed, her soft body cradled in my arms. Every few minutes, she looked up and smiled. Feeling safe and comfortable, she snuggled up again. She knew the song. She sang along, "*Ya Hay. Ya Hay.*" Then, she asked, "Nai Nai, what is E Ya Hay?"

"E Ya Hay is the same thing as Fa La La La or Ooby, Dooby Do."

She was happy knowing exactly what that meant. She looked at me again. Smiling pleasantly, confidently, slowly, and gently, she fell asleep. At last, this was the gratifying moment I was waiting for, a much needed and most desired snooze and rest time for my aching, old muscles.

Sandy was very smart and curious. She asked many questions and listened intently as I tried to answer or explain them plainly. When she started first grade, she became more aware of the real world. She quickly realized that not everyone treated her like a princess. Her wishes were not always granted. There were twenty other royal children in her class. She was no longer the favorite one.

At first, she was sad and seemed depressed. Gradually, she learned that she needed to step out of her safe and perfect world and adjust to the real one. As she observed and experienced new events, she would ask me how and why. At age six, she was very advanced with her vocabulary and very eager to learn and try new things.

I tried my best to describe what was going on around her and worked to enlighten her about what my life was like when similar events happened to me years ago and how Chinese people reacted and responded to these events.

Most importantly, I wanted to share with her our Chinese culture and traditions that have slowly been forgotten, morphed, or assimilated into western culture. My own children, Phoebe and Justin, were fortunate to have two sets of grandparents to enlighten and enrich their lives with Chinese culture and tradition. Phoebe even speaks fluent Mandarin. Justin can understand Mandarin and speaks broken Chinese.

Many of my friends and their American-born children don't know anything about how the Chinese people have struggled in China and in America. It has become my goal to remind the children of Chinese descent, like Sandy, that we, too, have unique and long-established customs. And no matter how good or bad they might be, they should not be consigned to oblivion.

CHAPTER 2

THE NEW IMMIGRANTS

In August 2022, nearly 40,000 migrants arrived in New York. They were being sent by bus from Texas by its governor. Some of them were staying in the hotel near where we lived. They were provided food and shelter. They were the lucky ones who survived a tumultuous and death-defying journey from their homeland.

Nearby our two-family house was the Oakland Lake. Sandy and I frequently enjoyed strolling along the lake and watching the magnificent swans gliding gracefully on the water. The lake always had visitors taking photos and some would even try their luck at fishing.

On one of those walks, we saw crowds of people, mostly speaking Spanish, congregating in the park. Sandy asked why there were so many people there.

"It was never this crowded before," said my six-year-old Sandy.

I took a deep breath and said sadly, "They are here because they were very lucky."

"Why are they lucky?" asked Sandy?

"They traveled from faraway countries to get here."

"Why are they here?"

"They want a better life," I said.

"What is a "better life?"

"A better life is not having to worry about food or shelter or being killed."

"But who wants to kill them?"

"Their government," I said.

"What's government?"

"It's like the king or emperor of a country."

"Why would the king want to kill people?"

"Some kings are corrupt and evil."

"Is our king evil?"

"No, America does not have a king. Our president is very kind. He helps everyone," I told her. "That's why so many people come here."

"Are these people going to stay in this park?" Sandy asked.

"No, they stay in the hotel and will move out soon and get a job somewhere."

"What's a job?"

"That's a thing you do every day so that you can get money to pay for food and housing."

"Oh yeah. Mom and Dad have jobs."

"Yes, they work hard so that you can have nice clothes to wear and lots of toys to play with."

"Did you have toys when you were little?"

"No, we had no toys," I answered. "My father worked very hard, but had no money to buy toys. Also, toys were not important for us back then. Very few toys were made."

I paused for a moment before I asked her the next question. "Did I ever tell you that I was an immigrant, like some of the people in the park?"

"What's an immigrant?"

"Immigrants are people who left their country and went to another country."

"What country did you leave to come here?"

"China. My father wanted my mama and my sister, your great aunt Tina, to leave our country, China. We were just like these foreigners who are here now. Great Aunt Tina was six years old, same as you are now."

"Why did your father want you to leave?"

"China did not have democracy like America. It was controlled by the communists."

"What?"

"In America people have choices. In China there are no choices at all."

"Choices for what?" Sandy was puzzled.

"Imagine that you want a new toy. In China, there are no toys except for wood sticks. In America, you can have dolls or trucks or sticks of all kinds. Which would you like?"

"Ahh, I like dolls with magic wands. Would I have that in China?" She was curious.

"Not in the 1950s. China has all kinds of dolls *now*, and at a very low price too."

"So, China is better now?"

"Only in certain things. People still have very little choice on what kind of religion or life they want for themselves. The good thing is that people are not starving in China anymore. But people are still very afraid of what they say or do. The government can put them in jail or put them to death."

"Oh, that's bad. That's why they want to come here?"

"Yes. Many governments want to kill their own people. Many people have no jobs back home and have to come here to find work," I explained.

The bigger story that I didn't share with Sandy then was that there was a lot of turmoil in China after World War II. There was a Civil War for control of the country, and the communists won, forming the People's Republic of China. That created much uncertainty and immeasurable fear. It threatened deaths and hardships for most people and forced many thousands of Chinese to flee China.

This was why my father insisted that Mama, my sister Tina, and I leave and not return. He was already experiencing oppression by the government. His business exporting Chinese porcelain vases and figurines was confiscated by the Communist Party. He wanted us to escape the brutal government and seek a better life in Hong Kong, which was a British colony then. The goal was to eventually make our way to America, where my maternal grandparents lived.

In the summer of 1959, Mama took Tina, who was six years old, and me on a train ride out of Shanghai. I was nine and had no idea that we would never see our father again. We would not return to Shanghai until 2005.

After we reached a small village in Quandong, a short and shabby looking man with a tattered fisherman's hat guided us toward Macau, a Portuguese colony. We climbed on foot through mountains in the dark, sleeping on straw in dilapidated shacks, and going to the bathroom in the woods. There were no hotels or restaurants. We had to travel in secret because this part of the journey to Macau was illegal. Likewise, going to Hong Kong, a British colony, was also illegal. We were being smuggled.

When we finally reached a beautiful white beach in Macau, the sky was gray with dark clouds. We were told that a boat would take us to Hong Kong that night.

I saw that there were two boys traveling by themselves. I was shocked that their parents had sent them on this difficult journey alone. My admiration for their courage and curiosity about their expedition led me to ask many questions. Our conversation kept us entertained while we anxiously waited for a fishing boat to transport us across the border.

There must have been sixty or more people waiting on the beach. The weather was horrible. Everyone saw the lightning flashes and heard the roaring thunder. The howling wind and torrential rain caused the waves to soar and crash ominously.

I asked Mama, "Why are we going now?"

"This is the best time. It will be okay," she said calmly.

"But Mama, you told us never to go out when there is lightning."

"Yes, but this is a special time. God is sending the Lightning God to protect us."

"Will the Lightning God protect us too?" the younger boy asked.

"Of course, just stay close to us. We will all go to Hong Kong safely," Mama said to comfort them.

"We are lucky to be traveling with you," the older boy said gratefully.

"What are your names?" my mother asked kindly.

"I am Gao Ti and my little brother is Shao Ti."

"Very nice to meet you. These are my daughters Anly and Tina. The four of you should stay together and go back to the hut to get out of the rain. I will call you when the boat comes."

We were the only children on this journey. We quickly ran back to the small, unlit, and ragged straw hut near the beach. The adults stood shivering on the beach, waiting and praying.

"It is so cold and wet. I don't understand why we must take a trip in this weather," I complained.

"It is the best condition," Gao Ti explained. "When there is a storm, the Coast Guard does not patrol as frequently. A small fishing boat can easily pass from Macau to Hong Kong without being noticed."

"Oh, I see, but will everyone be safe? The waves are so high," I said worriedly.

"The boat can handle the waves," Gao Ti assured me.

"Why are you traveling alone? Why don't your parents come with you?" I asked curiously.

"My father made this trip safely to Hong Kong a few months ago. We are going to meet him and our grandparents."

"What about your mother?"

"She will come in a few months when my father can pay for her fare. Is your father here?" he asked.

"No, he is staying in Shanghai with my brother and other sister. This trip is only for us three," I explained without really knowing the details.

"Do you want to eat an apple while we wait?" He took out several apples from a canvas bag that was hanging from his shoulder and offered them to his brother and us.

"Yes, thank you. We are so hungry. The last time we ate was two days ago."

The red apple was so crunchy, crispy, and juicy. I tried not to lose any drops of juice by licking each bite. It was the most delicious food that I have ever tasted. I ate it slowly and savored every bite.

"Come out, Anly, Tina, and boys," Mama called.

We ran to the beach and saw many men swimming to a fishing boat approximately forty feet long with its sails down. It was rocking back and forth, up and down, in the swelling waves. Anchored beyond a stretch of jagged rocks, it shook continuously as thunder, lightning, and torrential rain raged on.

"How are we going to get to that boat, Mama?" I asked with fear.

"Don't worry. They are going to put us in a smaller boat. Then, we can go onto that big boat," Mama calmly explained as she held us closely. The boys held tightly onto the edge of her long-sleeved blouse.

"Come here, come here, you children must go first. They need to sit in the bottom level of the boat," a man wearing a big rubber hat shouted loudly. He pointed to a small raft and demanded we children get in immediately.

The raft smelled. It was wet and dirtied with sand and seaweed. Ten people, made up of women and children, packed into the raft and someone pushed us off into the turbulent sea. The raft was then pulled toward the boat by some kind of tether. When we reached the fishing boat, which was really an old junk boat, a burly man in a black rubber poncho grabbed the boys. "Go, go down to the lower level," he shouted. His voice was as harsh as the howling wind.

He yelled and directed us children to descend through a square opening and into the lower level, which was the storage area for the day's catch. The dreadful stench of dead fish caused us to choke and gag. The floor was slippery with seawater. Tina and Shao Ti started to cry because of the darkness and the foul odor. They were sliding against other people due to the slick floor. As soon as more people crammed into the lower level, there was no room to slide or move at all.

Tina and Shao Ti were still crying. "I want to go home, Mama," cried Tina.

"We will be going to a nicer home soon," Mama said.

"I have to pee," Shao Ti said, crying.

"Oh, no. Hey mister, where can my children pee?" Mama asked the burly man in the rubber poncho.

"Ha! There is no place to pee. Just pee down there," he scoffed.

"But that is not sanitary. Everyone will be mad at my children."

"Don't worry, everyone will be peeing and puking soon." He laughed and covered the square opening with a black canvas.

The storage area was now pitch black. The labored breathing of dozens of people reverberated with severe coughing and deep gagging that was very stressful to hear. Shao Ti was crying more intensely as he grabbed his groin area and shouted, "I have to pee!"

Gao Ti took out the two remaining apples from the canvas bag and handed the empty bag to Shao Ti, "Go ahead. Pee in there." Shao Ti was trying to relieve himself and noticed that his urine went through the canvas bag and onto his feet.

"Oh, no. Oh, no. What should I do?" Shao Ti cried with panic and fear.

"Don't worry. Everyone understands. No one will yell at you," Mama said calmly as she stroked his hair.

"Who said that? Now, we have a stinky urine smell too. If I throw up, I will throw up on your head!" said another passenger in the dark.

Mama yelled back, "Will you all shut up? He is just a child. Stop screaming at my kids! Do you want the patrols to hear you?"

The boat was rocking more violently. It must have begun its dire mission. The tempestuous bouncing and shaking of the boat caused many people to become nauseous. It did not take long before Tina threw up. Shortly after, Shao Ti also heaved.

"Your children are disgusting! Now we are really in a stinky shithole," someone yelled.

"Stop complaining about my kids! According to the man on deck, you will all be peeing and puking soon. This shithole is for everyone. So, shut up!" Mama shouted back bravely.

Mama was thirty-three years old, five-foot three-inches tall, and weighed only about 100 pounds, but her menacing voice and the sheer anger piercing through her big eyes terrified them all.

Sure enough, no one complained anymore. They were all suffering from seasickness, including Gao Ti and me. Mama was busy trying to hold onto all of us and wiped our mouths with her soiled sleeves. The lower deck had become intolerable and unbearable to all.

We could hear the relentless rain beating on the canvas tarp. Rolling waves of seawater were seeping through the opening. An unexpected gust of strong wind blew the canvas off, and suddenly, a squall of very cold and wet breeze swooped in through the cargo hull. The wind was bone-chilling. The icy and piercing rain was painful and, at the same time, much welcomed. Everyone sighed as they breathed in fresh sea air. The horrible stench dissipated, if only for a few seconds.

The very fatigued and irritated burly man staggered over and placed the tarp over the cargo opening again.

"No, no, please leave the canvas off. We need fresh air. Please, the stench is killing us," said another passenger.

"Are you crazy? If I take the canvas off, this hole will fill with water. You will drown. Everyone will drown." He covered the opening and darkness resumed along with the reek of decay.

The repulsive odor was exacerbated by the agonizing sound of moaning and retching. The floor was filled with seawater, urine, and vomit. Tina was sobbing. Shao Ti was whimpering. I thought worms were crawling up my legs.

"Mama, I feel cold," Tina said softly as she shivered.

"Oh, no. You have a fever," Mama said after touching Tina's forehead. Then she checked all of us for fever. "Tina is so small, and her body can't take this terrible condition. We need to get off this boat."

"How are we going to do that?" Gao Ti asked.

"I don't know, but I'll ask," she raised her head and screamed loudly, "Hey mister! Hey mister! My daughter is sick. When can we get off this boat?" she repeated again and again.

"Now, you shut up. You are going to alert the patrols. We are probably almost there now," a very grumpy man complained.

"Your daughter is not the only one sick. My father is not breathing right. I think he is dying," said another person.

"Oh, no. We are all going to die!" someone yelled.

"Stop it! You crazy people are too loud," the drenched angry man said, lifting the canvas. Once again, everyone sighed with relief. Another violent blast of cold wind and icy rain swiftly brushed their faces. "We will get off soon," he said as he covered the opening again.

"Oh, good. We are almost there." Mama was happy. "I will find you some medicine when we get on shore."

Shao Ti and Tina were quiet, either from exhaustion or from hearing the good news. The moaning subsided as the others seemed to be comforted as well. The boat was still rocking. The unrelenting rain continued to beat the canvas tarp that was showing much wear and tear. A faint sliver of dim light seemed to be shining through.

It must be morning, I thought. I could see some daylight. Oh, Buddha, thank you. Thank the Emperor of Heaven and

Earth. Someone chanted a Buddhist prayer, *Na Mo A Mi Tuo Fo.*

We waited for what seemed like an eternity. No one seemed to mind the unbearable putrid air or the disgusting wetness anymore. Everyone's clothing was dirty and soiled, and their faces appeared sickly and ghastly. We were all looking forward to land and fresh air. Only the hope of a safe and clean landing sustained us.

The turbulent rocking of the boat seemed to have abated, and the boat slowed down. The engine was shutting down. Some people on the upper deck were cheering and clapping. We must be in Hong Kong. We made it!

The canvas was lifted again. At last, there was the much-needed sunlight and fresh air. Everyone was trying to get out of the cargo hull. Mama held us children tightly and told others to go first. We heard some people crying, "Oh, no. Oh, no."

"What could be wrong?" Mama said as she stood up and helped the children out of the cargo hull.

"Oh, no," she moaned.

"What happened?" Gao Ti and I both asked as we saw a dilapidated straw hut on the beach.

"This is not Hong Kong. This is where we started from," Mama said with disappointment.

"Stop whining. You are lucky you did not drown last night," the indignant brawny man howled at the passengers. "The storm was too violent. We will go again tonight."

After landing on the beach, everyone quickly rushed into the water to wash their faces and soiled clothing. The warm temperature of the water was so refreshing and the clothing quickly dried under the sun. It became clear what conditions were perfect for this type of travel. It had to be summertime when the water was warm, and it had to be done at night to avoid visibility by the coastal patrol. But couldn't it be done with a cleaner and less stinky boat?

"Are we going again tonight?" asked Gao Ti.

"I am not sure. I have to find a doctor for Tina. She is very sick," Mama said as she ran to speak with a short but taunting man wearing a shabby fisherman's hat made of straw. Apparently, he was the leader or organizer for this trip. Mama called him "Snakehead" because he was a slithering low-life who smuggled people across the border.

"What is wrong with Tina?" Gao Ti asked me.

"She tends to get sick very often."

"Why?"

"When she was born, she was two months premature and was very small and sickly. She is the reason why we are going to Hong Kong. Mama told me that we have to find doctors and medicines to help her."

"Oh, I hope she gets better soon. How is she going to go tonight?" asked Gao Ti.

"I don't know. But Mama will know what to do."

I saw Mama talking very seriously with Snakehead. She was stomping her feet and shaking her fists. The man pointed to an area beyond the hut.

Mama came back to get us all. "Let's go. There is a village not too far from here. We can find medicine and porridge." Mama carried Tina, and the boys and I walked slowly behind her away from the beach.

The so-called village was only a few dirt alleys filled with small shanty rooms. In one room there were pots of steaming buns and an old woman was yelling, "One tray, one Yuan." Mama put her hand into her pants pocket and took out some change and offered it to the merchant. The four of us were so famished that we ate quickly without noticing that Mama did not eat. There were only four small buns on the tray and five of us.

Mama asked the old woman where she could find a doctor or a herbalist. The merchant jeered and scoffed, "There are no healers in this hell. But there is a fortune-teller that we go to when we are sick."

"Why would you go to a fortune-teller?" Mama asked.

"He can tell you if you are going to die," she said nonchalantly.

"Does he have any healing herbs?"

"I don't think so," said the old woman.

"I don't need to see a fortune-teller. I need a doctor."

"Save your money. Go see the fortune-teller."

"Why?"

"If he says you are going to die, spend your money on a coffin. If he says you are going to live, spend your money on some wine. Once you are drunk, nothing hurts." She laughed, darkly.

We all went from door to door asking for information for an herbalist or where we could find Chinese herbs to lower Tina's fever. In a dark corner, on a square can that was used to store cooking oil sat an old man with long, gray, uncombed hair. His wrinkled face and blackened teeth made him look very frightening. He was smoking a pipe of sorts. He waved to Mama and said, "You are very brave. You are too beautiful to be in a place like this with four children. Someone will rape you and kidnap your sons."

"Master, can you please help us? My daughter is sick with a fever. I will pay you with this ring if you can give me some herbs to lower her fever." Mama showed the old man her ruby ring.

He examined the ring and said, "This stone is useless, but the gold is worth something." He sighed and yelled into the back of his tiny and dark room, "Lao Poa [*wife*], bring out some porridge and green tea." An elderly woman appeared with a small bowl of porridge and an even smaller cup of tea. The old man leaned over and whispered something into her ear. She hurried back in and then came out with a small alabaster ginger jar. The old man removed the lid and took out some weeds. He placed the weeds in the porridge. He looked at all of us and pointed to Tina. "Have her swallow these herbs with the porridge and then drink the tea."

"Are you an herbalist? What are you giving my daughter to eat?"

"Don't eat it! It is probably poison," said Gao Ti as he tried to block Tina.

The old man laughed. "I have these herbs to heal myself, so I can keep on telling fortunes. I don't need to poison you. You will die when you are supposed to die. This young girl is not dying for a long time. She was born in the year of the dragon. She has a very long and strong life ahead of her," the old man said as he looked at each one of us children.

"You were born in the year of the Tiger. You will be very busy, just like your mother, protecting many people," he said to me.

Then he paused for a moment. "Beautiful lady, these boys are not your sons," he said. "They are surrounded by ... hmmm. You must feed them something to eat so they don't go hungry."

Mama looked puzzled and surprised that the old man knew what year her daughters were born. She thought for a moment and then told Tina to eat the porridge and drink the tea.

Tina frowned and gagged. "No, it tastes bitter."

"It's okay. I think this elderly gentleman will not harm you," Mama said.

"You will need another dose tonight and tomorrow morning," the old man said as he took the ring from Mama. "This ring will pay for three doses."

"But we have someplace to go tonight," Mama urged.

"Your journey will begin in three days," he said calmly.

"What about us?" Gao Ti asked.

"Your journey continues. Eat something before going."

We went back to the beach, and Mama went looking again for Snakehead. She told him she wanted to postpone the scheduled trip for three more days.

"Are you crazy? Who do you think you are? You can't tell me when you want to go or stay. If you don't go tonight, someone else will take your place. You will forfeit your fare. You have no place to stay for three days. I can't guarantee there will be room for you in the boat three days from now." He yelled belligerently and stormed off cursing.

"What should we do?" I asked.

"We will wait and see if Tina is better. If she is better, we go. If she still has a fever, we stay."

"What about us?" Gao Ti asked nervously.

"I don't know how to reach your father in Hong Kong," Mama said. "I don't know if he would want you to stay with us. He might think that you were kidnapped and call the police."

Mama began to talk to herself. "I don't have enough money to stay here for three days. Why did the old man tell me three days? Should I listen to him? I am sure that damned Snakehead would want us to pay again if we don't go tonight." As Mama talked to herself, she removed her jewelry and stuffed them all in her pants pocket.

"I understand," Gao Ti said. He lowered his head and took Shao Ti's hand. "We will go tonight. We still have two apples. That is enough for us."

"No, the old man told me to feed you. We will go back to the village and eat something before we sail tonight. It is just windy, not raining yet, so hopefully the ride should be calmer. Besides, we will also go if Tina is better," Mama insisted.

We went back to the old woman who was steaming buns earlier that morning. She made us some dumplings. Mama had one dumpling and then started to ask different people where she could find shelter for three days. She also inquired about other ways to get to Hong Kong. Some men looked at her with lust. Some looked at her with pity. Some were indifferent and did not want to talk to her, a mere transient, here today, gone tomorrow.

After the meal, we went back to the fortune-teller. Tina forced down her second dose of bitter porridge and tea. The old man looked at us and said, "May Buddha watch over you tonight."

The night fell quickly. There was no moon or stars. The wind began howling again. The angry waves were once again crashing against the rocks and the beach.

Mama touched Tina's forehead and noticed the fever still lingered. She looked hesitant. Snakehead came and shouted, "Come on, children. You go first." He pulled at Tina and Shao Ti.

"Mama, I don't want to go. That boat smells awful," Tina cried.

"It's a different boat, stupid," Snakehead lied.

"It looks the same to me," Gao Ti said.

"Shut up. Either you go now or you forfeit your trip."

The boys looked at my mother and saw the painful tears in her eyes.

"Mama, let them stay with us," I begged.

"If we all forfeit our trip tonight, I need to pay for five more tickets later. I can't reach anyone for help right now." Mama started to cry.

"It's all right," Gao Ti said bravely. "There is no rain or thunder or lightning. It should be a better trip than last night. We will be fine. Thank you."

"May the Goddess of Mercy watch over you," Mama said, praying.

Gao Ti took his brother by the hand and walked confidently toward the same stinky raft. Their tiny heads bounced up and down until they reached the junk boat. Their little bodies quickly disappeared among the masses.

All the sails were hoisted and unfurled. The engine started, and the boat began to move. The monstrous waves were very fierce. The boat was again rocking and shaking. We were the only passengers who did not go. Snakehead and his crew were watching from the beach. We could see shadows of passengers bouncing up and down on the deck. Some seemed to be leaning over the edge of the boat to throw up.

"Oh no, Mama, I think that is the same boat we were on last night," I said as I held onto her tightly. "I hope they cleaned up the lower level."

"I am sure they did. They have to go out fishing today, so they must clean up all the garbage," Mama said with a frown.

"The boat smelled awful. It's not raining, so maybe they won't cover the hole. But look, the boat is rocking just as much as last night," I said.

"Hey girl, shut up! You are going to jinx the boat," Snakehead yelled loudly.

The sails were arched and spread fully as the boat was moving slowly away from the beach. I could see the boat shaking violently left and right. Snakehead walked away with another man, saying calmly, "Once they get past the rocks, they will be fine."

There was a very long and large body of jagged rocks to the right of the boat. The boat had to navigate beyond the rocks for safe passage. The sails were struggling violently against the untamable wind. The boat was rocking forcefully against the crest of the ferocious waves. I watched anxiously and did not want to leave. The boat managed to sail beyond most of the rocks.

Tina was getting seasick just watching the vigorous bouncing up and down of the boat. She gagged and threw up again, so Mama cleaned out her mouth and proceeded toward the hut. Suddenly, a thunderous crashing boom was heard. People on the beach gasped in horror. I turned quickly and gazed into the horizon. The boat had collided with the last bit of the treacherous stretch of rocks.

Mama instantly collapsed onto the sand. "Oh, no. Please, no!" she cried. I covered my mouth with shaking hands and stared in petrified shock.

Snakehead and other men dove into the sea and swam quickly toward the boat. There seemed to be many wooden structures and human figures falling into the sea. The sails toppled and the boat appeared to have snapped in two.

"Oh Gao Ti, please swim back to us," I prayed.

"*Na Mo A Mi Tuo Fo*, Goddess of Mercy, protect the boys," Mama prayed.

We repeated the prayer as we watched helplessly. We were not Buddhist, but it was the only prayer we knew. More and more of what seemed to be human figures were tossed into the air, then into the sea. The bow was sinking, the stern was cracking, and the center of the boat with the cargo hull was missing. Some distant and faint screaming and yelling could be heard. Snakehead and his men were almost there.

"Please, please, Goddess of Mercy, save them. They are just boys, too young to die," Mama said, continuing to pray. "It's my fault! I should have let them stay with me. Forgive me please!" She did not get up from the sand. She knelt and cried, clutching her broken heart.

"The fortune-teller said Buddha would watch over them," I comforted Mama.

"No. No. I think the fortune-teller knew they were going to die." Mama cried even more miserably.

"But he said I am supposed to protect many people. They will be fine," I said with some confidence.

"Not this time, my dear. Not this many people. Your life is just beginning. You will help others when you are older," Mama whispered as she took in a deep, slow breath. She stood up. We walked toward the water hoping to get a better view. The unforgiving and ferocious sea swallowed the boat and left the tip of the mast bobbing like a toothpick.

I lifted my head to the sky. "Whoever lives up there, Buddha, Goddess of Mercy, Heavenly Emperor, please don't take away my friends."

Mama was a pillar of strength and a pillow of comfort for my sister and me. Tina slept in Mama's lap and I leaned against Mama's trembling body. Mama and I kept vigil as we watched helplessly as Snakehead and his men pulled many bodies onto the beach. More and more villagers came out to help.

At the end of that horrific night, in the wispy purple haze of dawn, countless bodies laid lifelessly on the beach. The bodies of the boys were missing. The rescuers were exhausted. It was unfathomable that my family survived and others perished. I was angry and stupefied. "Why did you take them?" I yelled.

Snakehead kept shaking his head, sighing and chanting a Buddhist prayer, "*Na Mo A Mi Tuo* Fo." The other villagers were also mumbling some prayers under their breath.

I did not understand why Snakehead was still praying. Buddha did not help. The Goddess of Mercy did not help. The Heavenly Emperor wasn't there. My friends were gone. It was the first time that I ever felt so miserable, an unfathomable aching in my heart and an unexplained numbing in my limbs, but I didn't cry. I was angry, very angry. I didn't understand why Gao Ti was taken away. He was so generous. He gave us his apples. He was so brave. He took care of his brother. How could the almighty Emperor of Heaven and Earth be so merciless and snatch away the lives of two innocent boys?

Three Buddhist monks were summoned in the early morning, and they paraded around the bodies. One chanted as he counted his prayer beads. One was clanking a small brass bowl. One was drumming a wooden bowl with a fish carving. Villagers burned incense and nuggets made of gold and silver-colored paper as they prayed for the dead. I was frozen as I watched the solemn procession.

Snakehead walked slowly toward Mama. He shook and lowered his head. "There will be another boat tomorrow," he said softly with guilt.

"No, we are not going on any of these fishing boats," Mama answered sternly.

"The Emperor of Heaven and Earth did not want us to go on this kind of boat. There must be another way," Mama demanded. "My daughter saved our lives." Mama pointed to Tina.

"But there is no other way," Snakehead insisted.

"Do you know the fortune-teller in the village?"

"Yes," he answered.

"He knew this was going to happen. He told me to feed the boys so they would not become hungry spirits," Mama explained. "You know there will be hundreds of hungry spirits haunting you now. You can never sleep until you repent and do a charitable deed for redemption," she threatened.

"The fortune-teller did not predict this. He would have warned me," Snakehead said.

"Well, he warned us. He told me that my journey would happen two days from now. That is why I asked you yesterday to postpone my trip for three days."

"Really?" Snakehead asked with disbelief.

"He also said that my daughter was born in the year of the dragon. This is not her time to die. My older daughter was born in the year of the tiger. She will protect us. We were spared for a reason." Mama spoke loudly so everyone on the beach could hear her.

Many villagers bowed to us and burned more incense. The monks nodded to Snakehead. A sudden fear appeared in his squinty eyes.

"I will try. It will cost more money," he said humbly.

"This is all I have." Mama gave him her necklace, bracelet, and watch. "You will get us to Hong Kong safely or else these hungry spirits will come for you," Mama said fiercely.

"Yes, yes. I will try my best."

"No, you will not *try*. You will *do* it!" Mama was now shouting.

We then went back to the village to get the last dose of the herbal porridge. We passed the old woman who sold buns. She offered us two trays of buns. "I told you to see the fortune-teller. He knows everything." Mama shook her head to decline the buns and said she had no money left. The old woman said, "No need. You paid yesterday."

Another woman saw my sister and me walk by. She quickly went inside and came out with two dresses for us. "You need to look good," she said. The villagers were in awe of our survival, believing that we were special, blessed beings.

The fortune-teller smiled and said, "Don't worry about the boys. They will never go hungry again. They are happy in heaven."

"How do you know that they will be fine?" I asked.

"I just know. You will be fine too. You will go far, very far from here."

"How will we get to Hong Kong? Snakehead said there is no other way." Mama was very concerned.

"Don't worry. You will go in a big boat."

"Not a fishing boat?" Mama said nervously.

"No. A bigger boat with lots of people wearing fancy clothing," he replied.

Snakehead came to the hut the next day and arranged for us to go by bus to another city. He gave Mama three tickets and told us not to talk to anyone, especially on the boat. The bus dropped us off at a pier where a gigantic ship with three decks was anchored. It was a tourist cruise ship.

The passengers were all well-dressed and had clean, shiny shoes. Tina and I were wearing new dresses, but our shoes were soiled and showed a great deal of wear. Mama was still wearing her very wrinkled and dirty long-sleeved blouse. Her scruffy pants were ripped and stained with black and brown spots. Although we might have looked slovenly, Mama walked with her head held high and smiled gloriously as we embarked on the beautiful ship that took us to safe harbor.

Whenever I eat an apple now, I think of Gao Ti and how my new life began on that dreadful stormy summer night. Many lives were lost. But we survived and continued onward to Hong Kong, where we stayed for three years. Like the fortune-teller predicted, we would go far, very far, from China. In 1962, we arrived in New York City.

Tina, Mama and Me 1959

Photos of Arrival in 1962 at Idlewild Airport,
NY (Currently called the JFK Airport)

CHAPTER 3

MY FATHER

Sandy was shocked and speechless after I told her about how we were spared from drowning. "Do all the immigrants go through scary trips like you did?" She was very worried.

"Some did, some did not." I comforted her as I saw the fear in her eyes. She was not ready for the tragedies in the real world. We went to her room to play with dolls and did not discuss the immigrant issues anymore.

Then, on Father's Day 2023, when she was seven years old, she surprised me with a question, "What happened to your father, after you left China, Nai Nai?" Sandy asked.

It was shocking to me that she remembered about my father. I took a deep breath and sighed. Tears swelled in my eyes. How should I tell her the story of my father? "My father, your great-grandfather, Jensen, was badly treated by the Communist Chinese."

"Who are they and why?"

"The Communists are a government where people must do what their leader says. The people have no choice. What would you say if you were told that you can only play with small wooden sticks, not metal ones, not colorful or big ones, and no dolls or anything else?"

"That would be terrible. I don't like that. Do people really follow these rules?"

"They have to. If they don't, they will be punished or killed."

"That is awful. I don't like that at all."

"Great-grandfather Jensen did not want to follow the Communist government either. He was punished and badly treated," I explained and continued to enlighten Sandy of the horrible treatment that my father endured after we left Shanghai.

My father attended the Whampu Military School in Nanjing and became one of the accountants for the Kuomintang, the ruling Nationalist Party of China. He was a supporter of General Li Zongren, who was once a warlord, became a general, and then the vice-president of the Republic of China, right-hand man to Chiang Kai-shek. When the Nationalists lost the civil war to the Communists in 1949, many Nationalist members left China with their leader, Chiang Kai-shek, the president of the Republic of China, and retreated to Taiwan.

"Are the Nationalist the good guys?"

"The Nationalists would allow children to play with toys if you can afford them. They gave the people a choice."

Some members of the Nationalist party remained in China, believing that the Nationalists would eventually co-exist with the Communists. In fact, General Li Zongren was trying to broker a peace deal with the Communists before the latter officially established the People's Republic of China in 1949.

In addition to being an accountant, my father was a successful businessman in Shanghai who owned a factory that produced porcelain vases and figurines. Many other successful businessmen in the country stayed in the newly established country because of their careers. My father decided to stay as well, as he had a business and did not want to lose all of his possessions and start anew on a strange island, Taiwan, with no promise of employment.

After the Nationalists left China, the Communists tried to implement industrial and economic reforms. However, the Korean War was raging on and the Communist Party was supporting the North Koreans. Supporting this war in addition to rolling out new nationwide reforms caused major devastation to the new Communist Chinese economy.

In particular, Mao Zedong, the leader of the Communist Party, wanted total control over the production of all the grains being farmed in China. Hence, Mao initiated "cleansing campaigns" to identify once wealthy or former members of Kuomintang or the Nationalists who owned land. These targeted people had their land taken and then were sent to poor farming villages to assist as laborers as a form of "re-education". Most of them were assigned the most important job, shoveling human waste and bringing it to the fields as fertilizer.

My father was initially spared this humiliation. His business was very successful, and he was able to support our extended family. When my grandmother joined my grandfather in the US in 1949, they left behind their two sons, aged eleven and nine, with Mama. We called them big and little uncles. My grandparents knew that my parents would be able to care for them without any financial problems. My father also provided for his former wife and three children in Hubei province. He always took good care of our family of six. My big uncle was able to attend college in Beijing, with my father's financial support. My little uncle left Shanghai to go to Hong Kong in 1957, also under my father's auspices. Little uncle later came to America in 1959.

Mama in 1955 with her two younger brothers and four children

During the early fifties, my father owned a house in Shanghai where we all lived very comfortably. It was a three story, five-bedroom house with indoor plumbing. In fact, we were the only house in the neighborhood with indoor plumbing because the previous owner was a French diplomat who imported the modern plumbing designs from Europe. Mama was able to hire one servant to care for us while she worked as a nurse.

As the years of communist rule progressed, though, the Communists would periodically identify my father as a former Kuomintang member and pro-Nationalist. They would send my father to a labor camp on a remote island and make him dig and dig to ready the earth for a train track. Thank God, my father was not shoveling human waste. Although, as I think about it now, it could be that he did shovel human waste and told us a different story because he did not want us to know.

When the communists needed more money, they confiscated my father's factory and made it government owned. My father was a respected boss one night and became a disrespected and disgraced worker the next day.

With this change in his fortune and a political target forever on his back, my father realized that his life was doomed and did not want the rest of his family to suffer the same. He encouraged Mama to apply for a traveling visa to Hong Kong and leave Shanghai. The Chinese government required traveling documents for anyone leaving a city. Mama also needed the hospital in which she worked to grant her permission to travel from Shanghai to Guangdong. Going from Guangdong to Macau, then to Hong Kong, was totally illegal and must be done at night, guided by a human smuggler. My father gave Mama all his money and gold to arrange for the legal passage from Shanghai to Guangdong and for the illegal passage to Hong Kong.

My tiny sister, Tina, had lost so much weight when she contracted chickenpox. Due to the outstanding work Mama did in the hospital, she was able to get many medications to treat Tina. However, Tina's continued illness provided the best reason for my mother to leave Shanghai seeking better medical consultation.

Both Mama and my father wanted my brother Kyle to leave China as well. However, they feared that the government would become suspicious that they were trying to smuggle out their firstborn son and deny all our applications to leave China. Mama used Tina's chronic illnesses and my own kidney problems to ascertain our visas to travel to Hong Kong. Only the three of us would be able to leave China. It would be seventeen years until I saw my brother, Kyle, and the youngest sister, Jade. I never saw my father again.

Father, Kyle and Jade 1960

Mama was heartbroken, leaving her firstborn son and her youngest daughter behind. My dad promised to rehire the wet nurse who took care of Kyle at birth to come and help care for the children. Mama promised to find work in Hong Kong and send money home.

After we left Shanghai, my father's life and fortune continued to suffer. He paid a hefty and painful price for remaining in the country. He was willing to bear any punishment that the brutal communist government would levy. He had already been arrested, humiliated, beaten, stoned, spat upon, and "re-educated" multiple times. He knew and did not care that he would be arrested again.

No one could have foreseen the deadly Cultural Revolution that Mao Zedong initiated in 1966. This "revolution" labeled anyone too intellectual or too successful as a counter-revolutionary or an imperialist. These perceived threats to the new Communist ruling party were now to be subject to multiple rounds of public humiliation, which the government deemed as "re-education." The idea behind this dehumanizing practice was that humiliating these counter-revolutionaries would make them humble and obsequious.

Of course, with my father's business background and political ties, the government labeled him as a counter-revolutionary, right-winger, *and* an imperialist. The term traitor was eventually added to that list, because Mama did not return to Shanghai, which was considered an act of treason.

During this time, the Red Guards commandeered my father's five-bedroom house and allowed him only two rooms. He had to share his entire house with strangers and a kindergarten school which took over the entire first floor and the courtyard. One of the two rooms was occupied by my big uncle, Mama's younger brother, so technically, my dad only had one room to his name. All his worldly possessions and expensive red wood furniture were confiscated.

He was tortured and assaulted throughout the many different "cleansing and corrective campaigns" that the communist government implemented. He had to write posters for all to see, confessing to all his supposedly shameful lifestyles and beliefs.

The "merciful" communists would not kill him. They preferred torture. The government wanted him kept alive so that he could be frequently and publicly displayed on the main streets and be humiliated as a member of the Five Black Categories, which included landlords, rich farmers, bad influencers, counter-revolutionaries, and right-wingers. My siblings Kyle and Jade were also displayed, standing alongside my father. They, too, suffered being spat on, sneered, and jeered. Kyle and Jade were sent to far-away farming villages to be "re-educated". Kyle was not allowed to attend college or join the army even though he passed all the qualifying examinations. Jade contracted Malaria and her hands and feet were horribly scarred from working in the dirty rice paddies. After years of abuse, my father suffered a severe stroke in 1972 and became paralyzed. Kyle and Jade were allowed to return to Shanghai to care for him. He died in 1974 of a massive stroke, in the only room that the government allowed him to keep in what was once his own house.

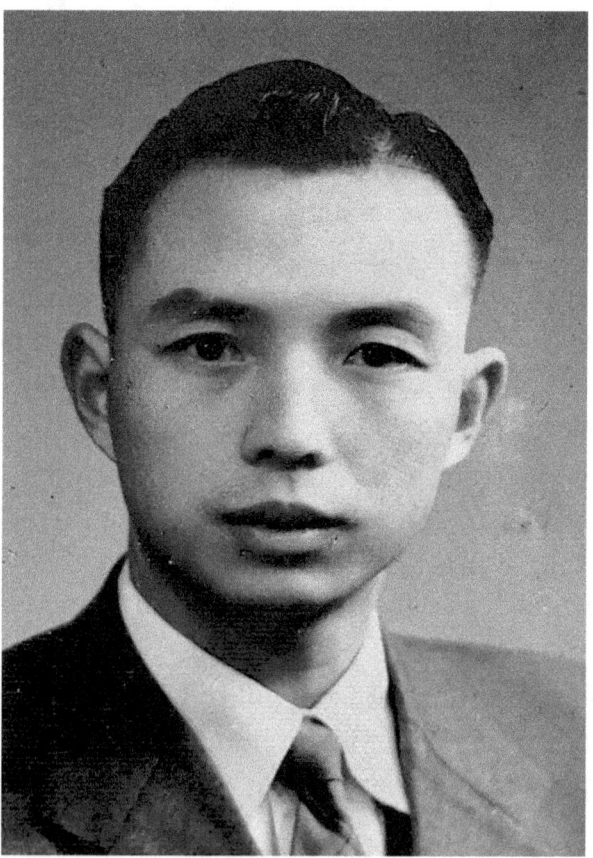

Photo of My Father

CHAPTER 4

MY GRANDPARENTS

Living in a two-family house is great for us. Sandy and I visit each other very frequently each week. One day, she saw on the television news broadcast that many immigrants were being moved out of overcrowded New York City hotels to a newly constructed encampment area in Randall Island.

"Nai Nai, when you first came here to the US, did you live in a hotel?" Sandy asked.

"What hotel? It wasn't a hotel. We lived with my grandparents in a very small and crowded living room of a tiny one-bedroom apartment."

"Nai Nai, how did your grandparents come here?"

"My grandpa came to America on a scholarship."

"Your grandpa came here for school?"

"Well, yes and no."

"What do you mean?"

"I have to tell you a little bit of history about China and America in order for you to understand how my grandfather, your great-great-grandfather, came here in 1926."

"History? What's that?"

"History is a true story from the past."

"I love stories. Please tell me about your grandfather."

A long time ago, in the 1800s, China was a country far away from the Western world. People from the West did not understand the Chinese customs and vice versa. However, Chinese people were impressed by the intelligence and elegance of the British people. They welcomed these foreigners and traded with them for a long time.

The British and other European countries loved the huge market provided by the most populous country in the world. They liked the jade, silk, porcelain, and various teas from China. The Chinese, on the other hand, were interested in Western textiles, fur, glassware, metalware and of course, opium, which was illegal to import.

The introduction of illicit opium to China was disastrous. Addiction spread throughout the country. The Chinese government fought two wars to rid China of opium from Britain and France. China lost both of these wars, had to pay reparations, ceded Hong Kong to the British Empire, and was forced to trade with Britain and France under terrible tariffs.

Meanwhile, in 1882, the US Congress passed the Chinese Exclusion Act. Chinese people were not allowed to immigrate to the US for almost forty years.

The Boxer Rebellion of 1900 was another attempt by the Chinese government to rid China of foreigners and their unfair trade practices. The "boxers," armed with their highly trained martial arts (Chinese boxing is what Westerners called martial arts at the time), were clearly outmatched by the Westerner's firepower and advanced ammunition. China once again lost the war against foreign powers including Russia, the United States, Japan, Britain, and four other countries. China was again forced to pay exorbitant reparations to these countries.

In 1924, the Chinese Exclusion Act was revised with severe quota restrictions. Only two percent of the Chinese population would be allowed to immigrate from China. The Chinese population was based on the 1890 US census. My grandfather was a very brave and intelligent man. When he heard of this very limited opportunity, he immediately applied for a student visa to come to the US. He paid for his own transportation and lodging. The tuition was then waived by the University of Illinois due to the funds set aside by the Boxer Rebellion Indemnity Scholarship. The US established this scholarship with the excess reparation funds, $11 million, that was overpaid by China to America as reparations for the Boxer Rebellion.

Grandfather was encouraged by his family to explore the world. Grandmother was expected to stay at home in China to master cooking, embroidery, and sewing. When my grandfather came to America as a student in early 1926 at age twenty-seven, he brought with him many carved soapstone sculptures to sell to pay for his transportation and expenses.

To his surprise, all the sculptures that he had brought over from China sold very quickly. He immediately telegraphed my grandmother and asked her to send more. This interest by Westerners began his business of importing Chinese arts and crafts. Instead of studying at the University of Illinois that provided the scholarship for him, he became a businessman. He went back to China to bring back more soapstone carvings and other arts and crafts.

After twenty years of traveling back and forth to China to bring back more antiques, jewelry, and sculptures, he finally settled down in New York City and started a full-time wholesale import business. When the Chinese Exclusion Act was finally repealed in 1946, Grandpa was able to apply for a visa to sponsor grandma to come to New York in 1949. They had been living on two separate continents for twenty years.

Finally, they were able to live together. However, they had to leave behind their two precious sons.

In those days, a sponsor had to verify they had at least $5,000 in a savings account. They were then responsible for the food, shelter, and livelihood of the immigrant they sponsored, because new immigrants were not eligible for any government handouts or programs that US citizens were. The immigrants today, however, could and would receive many benefits.

While Grandpa did things by the books, there were many male immigrants who came to New York City illegally. They would find laborious work and marry someone who was a citizen. Then they would pay for the women's living expenses for five years to be able to get a permanent resident card.

Some clever women made getting these much-sought-after green cards into a very profitable, no-hassle business by marrying the man for a certain amount of money and then divorcing him immediately after the green card was obtained. The women were free to marry again to make even more money. Meanwhile, these women continued to work at their normal jobs and never had to share their bedrooms with their on-paper husbands.

My grandpa would help the new immigrants earn a living by calling a few Chinese restaurant owners and asking about job vacancies. Usually, someone would need a waiter or a dishwasher. If no openings were available, he would show the new immigrants how to peddle Chinese slippers, lanterns, and other novelties. He would pack two shopping bags full of merchandise from his wholesale shop and tell the newcomers which train to take and where to get off, usually Times Square, Herald Square, or Union Square, to find customers for the products. They would then find a clean street corner and lay down a cloth to display the Chinese slippers and lanterns for sale.

People passing by would be attracted to the beautiful and exotic items and pay one dollar for each without haggling. When the bags were empty at the end of the day, they returned to grandpa's store and paid him for the cost of the merchandise sold and bought more for the next day.

Who knew that Grandpa's was the first charitable organization founded in a small one-bedroom railroad apartment on 28th Street and 2nd Avenue in Manhattan to help new Chinese immigrants? The news of his kindness and generosity spread quickly and countless new faces, total strangers, became street-peddling entrepreneurs with the help from Grandpa's no-deposit, no-interest, sell-first-pay-later business loans.

One old couple in particular, both very thin, frail, and hunched over from osteoporosis, benefited the most from Grandfather's business loan. We called them Chu Gong Gong and Chu Po Po which meant grandparent Chu. They did not want to compete with other peddlers in Manhattan. Instead, they traveled to Flushing, Queens to peddle their slippers. They found a corner next to a coffee shop that was located under a train overpass. The location was perfect for them; they were shielded from the rain and the snow.

They became very friendly with the owner of the coffee shop, who was a kind middle-aged man who sold newspapers, candy, sandwiches, and beverages. He allowed the old couple to sell the slippers outside his store and permitted them to use the shop's restrooms when needed. Chu Gong Gong bought one sandwich to share with his wife each day from the store owner.

Since the old couple looked very weak, emaciated, and vulnerable, they attracted sympathy from the onlookers and passersby. That enabled them to sell a lot of the merchandise Grandpa imported, such as silk fans, silk scarves, and small vases.

The coffee shop owner and the old couple continued their friendly relationship for five years. Then, one day, the coffee shop owner told them, "You need to go somewhere else soon."

"Why? You no like us no more?" the old man asked.

"No, that is not it." The coffee shop owner sighed. "I am closing my store."

"Why? Business no good?" The old man was puzzled.

"No, my landlord wants to sell the building."

"What landlord? You no landlord?"

"No, I rent. My lease is expiring next month," said the store owner. "The landlord is not renewing my lease. He is selling the building. You have to find somewhere else to sell your stuff. The new owner will not let you sell here."

"Why? I bother nobody."

"I know, but I really don't think the new owner likes peddlers in front of the building."

"Where you going? You go new place?"

"Yeah. I'll find something." He lowered his head and went inside his store.

Chu Gong Gong discussed this very serious dilemma with his wife, who told him to explain the problem to my grandpa, who had a very loyal customer who loved the ivory and cloisonné merchandise that grandpa imported. That customer also happened to be a lawyer, and he quickly found the name of the owner of the building and negotiated the sale of the building.

A few months later, the coffee shop owner had a new lease, allowing him to stay open. The old couple was able to continue their humble peddling of merchandise that Grandpa imported. The new owners of the building did not mind the peddling because the old couple had used all of their hard earned savings and became the new owners of the building!

Even after they became the owners, they continued to work hard peddling crafts throughout the year. It took them another three years to save enough money to sponsor their son and grandson to immigrate from the countryside of China to America.

Grandpa never earned any commission or interest from them or anyone else's sales. He was always helpful to all those who came to him. He would lend money to the new immigrants and gave credit to many peddlers who could not pay him back. His business was set back and lost a great deal of money when his shop was burned to the ground due to an electrical fire.

He never gave up, continued to work hard, and had great visions of what merchandise would be profitable. He tried selling many different items, and even ventured into making jewelry and lamps.

Besides importing Chinese gift items, he made custom lamps. He bought lamp kits that included the harp, the ornamental top, the socket, and electric cord. Then he drilled holes into the base of Chinese vases and wooden stands, adding wiring and a light bulb. He could make any vase a customer wanted into a beautiful lamp. Of course, in order to sell it at a good price, Grandpa needed my grandma to make a silk lampshade to complement the lamp.

My grandma was a very good seamstress and cook. Grandma sewed the silk lampshades to accompany the lamps that Grandpa made. The lamp and lampshade were a highly in-demand product but were very time-consuming to produce.

Customers handpicked the Chinese vases to be made into lamps and then ordered handmade silk lampshades. Grandpa took many orders for the lampshades and Grandma made them when she was not cooking or playing mahjong. She kept the money she made as her private savings and hid it from Grandpa. Sometimes, she would fold a hundred-dollar bill and sew it into the hem or a pocket in the lining of her Chinese dress, known as a *qipao*.

But Grandpa knew exactly which dresses had the cash. They were always the old and ugly qipaos that Grandma did not wear anymore.

Grandma was a wonderful and skillful cook. She welcomed all newcomers to share meals with us. Strangers who just arrived in New York would seek her out. They usually came with nothing and ate meals with us until they could find a job, usually with help from Grandpa. My grandma's tiny apartment was the first soup kitchen for Chinese immigrants.

In the 1960s, there were no supermarkets in Chinatown, which consisted of only three streets—Canal, Mott, and Bayard. My grandma would take me from store-to-store to buy the meats and vegetables she needed for her meals. Some of the stores were in the basements of buildings. Grandma would lean over the staircase and shout down to the merchant below.

"Hey, Little Brother, do you have any pork shoulder?"

"Yes, Auntie, how many pounds do you need?"

"Three pounds, and could you cut them into small pieces."

"Ok. I will bring it up to you. Don't come down."

Grandma and I would wait on the steps for the butcher to bring up the pork. I wondered, *What is going on in that basement? Do they chop up the pig right there? How bloody and dirty is the floor?* I was too afraid to find out. Grandma also told me that some of the buildings had tunnels in their basements. They were used to smuggle drugs between Chinatown and the near-by neighborhood called Little Italy.

One shopping occasion that still makes me laugh occurred in a poultry store. The chickens and ducks were freshly killed each day. Grandma picked out a four-pound chicken and told me to pay for it. The merchant charged us for five pounds. I asked why, and he said the extra pound was for the feathers.

"What feathers? I don't see any feathers."

"You don't see them because we plucked them already."

"Why are you charging for feathers that you throw away?"

"It's my labor you are paying for."

"Well, if I am paying for the feathers, then, give me the feathers. I can use them."

Grandma came in quickly to end the dispute. She apologized to the butcher and said, "She just got here from Hong Kong. She does not know how to buy chickens."

These days, freshly butchered chickens are wrapped in plastic and sold at a higher price, which probably includes the labor to kill and to pluck off one pound of feathers.

The most memorable shopping experience I remember was going with Grandma to an American seafood store around the corner from her building. Grandma spoke very little English, and the merchant did not speak any Chinese. However, between pointing, nodding, and finger-counting, Grandma always got what she needed.

This time, Grandma wanted to buy crabs. She walked in and looked and looked. There were no crabs, but there were some lobsters. She pointed to the lobsters and nodded. The merchant held up one finger, then two, and then three. Grandma shook her head, still pointing at the lobsters.

"Do you want the lobsters?" he asked, a little confused. Grandma shook her head. "What do you want?"

She pointed at the lobsters and raised her two hands. She mimicked the gesture of cutting by using her pointer finger and her middle finger, and then held up one hand pretending to cut with her finger-scissors.

The merchant asked, "You only want the claws?" He picked up one lobster and pointed to the claws and shook his head. "I can't sell just the claws."

Grandma looked at him and pointed to the claws. She then nodded and, facing the merchant, walked slowly toward the door, sideways. Both the merchant and I were puzzled. We watched Grandma walking sideways as she used both of her two-finger-scissors and pretended to cut in the air.

Oh My God, I said to myself. My dearest grandma was pretending to be a crab, walking sideways and waving her "claws" in the air. The merchant first looked shocked and then laughed loudly. "Ah, you want crabs! Sorry, I don't have any today. Come back tomorrow."

For years afterward, Sandy and I often both pretended to walk sideways like a crab, with our finger claws waving in the air like Grandma did, laughing hysterically while we did it.

Photo of My Grandparents

CHAPTER 5

ATLANTIC CITY

Sandy always brought her doll of the day and her favorite once-pink-now-gray velour bunny when she visited me. The velour bunny had since lost half an ear. No matter how tattered and aged the bunny was, it was still her best friend. On one occasion, she also brought her pajamas and toothbrush.

"Hi, Nai Nai. I am sleeping over. Yay!"

"I am so happy that you are staying with me for two nights. We will have so much fun," I said.

"I don't understand why I can't go with Mom and Dad," Sandy said sadly.

"They are going to Atlantic City for a convention."

"What's a convention?"

"A convention is a big meeting with lots of people."

"But isn't there a pier with an amusement park for kids?" Sandy asked.

"That's the new Steel Pier. It went through many changes over the years, burned down, and then was rebuilt."

"Did you ride on the Ferris wheel?"

"No. There wasn't a Ferris wheel when we were there."

"What was there?"

"We watched horses diving into the ocean," I said.

"What? Horses? Diving? Did they die?"

"No, they did not die, Sandy. Atlantic City was very different sixty years ago. There were no casinos then. No outlet stores either. But the Convention Center was there. Let me tell you all about what I saw back then."

When we arrived in New York City in 1962, my grandfather took my sister, Tina, and me to Atlantic City to help him in his seasonal gift shop, which was only open during the summer months. It was the first time that we had ever seen half-naked people running on the white sand beaches, proudly displaying their physiques for all to see.

The best part of the boardwalk experience happened at night. Contrary to their daytime beach attire, or lack thereof, the half-naked people transformed and were all dressed up in the evening. The ladies wore high heels and puffy skirts. The gentlemen wore jackets and long trousers. They strolled slowly together and enjoyed the sights and sounds of the boardwalk.

The aroma of fresh corn popping, peanuts roasting, and chocolate melting was extremely intoxicating. Tourists lined up and eagerly paid to see the famous black stallions jump from a height of 40 feet into a gigantic water tank at the Steel Pier. Nearby, some small pavilions had musicians playing live music. As always, there were many Madame X's and Y's who would tell people their fortunes for fifty cents.

"Seabiscuit" Steel Pier's Diving Horse, Lake County
Museum, Curt Teich Collection. Postcard

At age twelve, I was trained by my grandfather to be an entrepreneur. Every evening, I held in my hand a few packages of heel protectors. I scouted and waited for a damsel in distress. When a woman wearing high heels got her heels stuck in the crevices between the planks of the boardwalk, I rushed to her side and helped her pull the heel out of the cracks. Then, I asked my potential customer if she would like to put the heel protectors on to avoid this problem in the future. The ladies were usually very happy to see me and happily paid twenty-five cents for the heel protectors. That's how I learned that I could sell something, make money, and maybe even become rich someday.

Tina was only nine years old and was the best sales girl. With her dimpled, smiling face and newly permed curly hair, she resembled a Chinese Shirley Temple. Mama thought we would look more American if we had our hair permed before arriving in America.

Tina was always asked about the price of the items she was selling. She held a foldable paper fan in one tiny hand and five postcards in another. "A quarter, a quarter! Great buy!" she would say happily. Nine out of ten times, she would sell the foldable fan, which was a very timely and convenient item.

When I was not selling heel protectors at night, I would sell wooden puzzle boxes during the day. I would show a box to a male tourist and ask if he could open it. Grandpa told me not to bother the female tourists with this item because, he claimed, "Only men like to work with their hands."

The men would try to open the boxes, first while laughing and then more seriously. These boxes required several steps before they could be opened. Ninety percent of the time, I had to show them how to do it. They almost always bought the box they could not open at first.

But I was not just selling heel protectors and puzzle boxes. Grandpa told me the story of Jiang Tai Gong (姜 太 公) so I could learn to sell the porcelain figures of Chinese fishermen.

Jiang Tai Gong was a very wise man and a military strategist in the Zhou dynasty that lasted nearly 800 years and ended in 256 BC. He would sit by the bank of a river and fish in a very unusual and incomprehensible manner. His long fishing pole extended over the water, and the hook at the end of a long fishing line was above the water as well.

"How do you catch any fish if your hook is above the water?" asked many passersby.

"If the fish wants to be caught, it will jump out of the water and onto my hook," he said.

"That's impossible. You will never catch any fish. You will starve," they told him.

To everyone's surprise, every so often, a fish would jump out of the water and miraculously get hooked. The fisherman became famous for his incredible technique and unique insight. Villagers would come to him every day, speak with him, and ask him many questions. The fisherman would advise the villagers on how to solve their problems.

Before long, the news of this wise fisherman, with his hook above water, traveled throughout the land. The emperor soon heard about the wisdom of this fisherman and summoned him to court. The royal guards returned without the fisherman, which angered the emperor.

"Why would he not come see me? I can offer him gold and silver."

"He does not want gold and silver," the guards said.

"Well, what does he want?"

"He told us, 'If the emperor really wants to see me, he can come to me.'"

"What arrogance! Bring him here and cut off his head!" yelled the emperor.

"But the villagers all respect him. If he were killed, there would be unrest among the people," the guards said.

"Who would go see an old fisherman?"

"Many people from all over the country have traveled great distances to see him."

"Why?"

"Because they think the fisherman understands their problems and can help to solve them," the guards said.

"What?" asked the emperor, exasperated. "People think he is smart?"

"Yes, people think he is very smart, and they respect his advice."

"If he is *that* smart, then maybe he can help this court with the barbaric King of Shang that is threatening our land," said the emperor.

The country was shell shocked when they heard that the mighty ruler of their country, Emperor Zhou, left his comfortable and luxurious palace to travel to the poor fishing village.

The whole country was eagerly awaiting the meeting. Many villagers stood by the river in an effort to see the emperor. Before his arrival, the village was cleaned and the road was cleared of all debris and weeds. Finally, the elaborate and enormous royal entourage arrived.

Everyone expected the fisherman to humble himself and beg for forgiveness. Instead, the fisherman greeted the emperor with, "What question do you have for me?"

"What? How dare you? Who do you think you are?" yelled the emperor.

"I am the person whose advice you seek."

"What advice? I was just curious to see what you look like and why people think you are smart."

"People who need wise counsel will seek me out," said the fisherman. "They travel from near and far just to ask for my advice."

"And your advice is as good as gold?" asked the emperor.

"Gold is not that important," he replied.

"What could be better than gold?" The emperor was shocked.

"A peaceful long life with good health is much better," said the fisherman.

The emperor paused and took a step back to ponder the wisdom of this simple but very intelligent and philosophical man.

"Do you want my advice on how to deal with the King of Shang?" the fisherman asked.

"How did you know that?" The emperor was stunned by the question and impressed with the fisherman's knowledge of current events.

"Why else would you leave your glorious palace and travel this far unless you wanted some words of wisdom regarding an important issue. The only issue important enough for you to come to me is the safety and prosperity of your kingdom," the fisherman reasoned.

The emperor was impressed that the fisherman was indeed very knowledgeable and understood his dilemma. He brought the fisherman to his palace, and the military strategies devised by the fisherman helped the emperor defeat the King of Shang and expand the Zhou dynasty.

I would always end this story by saying, "You should always strive to be like the fisherman. Gather and hone great knowledge and skill. Then, you can sit quietly while others travel far and wide to seek you out." This story would almost always yield a sale, as everyone wanted to be like the fisherman, wise and sought after. The fisherman figurines were a particular favorite for the tourists who were doctors or lawyers, who indeed did sit in their office, while others traveled many miles and paid lots of money to seek out their professional advice!

Throughout the summer, I was in charge of keeping a record of daily sales in my grandpa's store. Using some of the money to shop at the local Acme grocery store was also my job. We would take one of the many free-of-charge jitneys that lined the streets off the boardwalk and go to Acme to shop once a week for the food we needed.

One of the cashiers in the store was a tall young man who was always happy to help us and did not mind that we paid with lots of coins. We always waited in his line. One time, he pointed out that a carton of milk we chose was leaking. He said, "Go and get a good container. I will wait for you."

He would patiently count the coins and put them in his cash drawers. He then gave us lots of stamps to stick on the Acme stamp book. The stamp books allowed us to trade the stamps we collected for merchandise. Nowadays, supermarkets give out bonus points instead of stamps.

On the boardwalk, we had one neighbor who sold soft ice cream and another who sold pizza. They offered us their products whenever my grandmother gave them some of her delicious home-made egg rolls. Tina and I loved the ice cream. It was a combination of chocolate and vanilla. The seller called it the "Twin Kiss." It took us a long time to get accustomed to the taste and smell of the strange looking triangular orange, red, and white bread called pizza. We had never seen it before, but we grew to love it.

Grandmother only stayed for a week or two every summer. Then, she would go back to Manhattan, leaving my sister and me to help our grandfather throughout the summer. She taught me how to cook and do laundry in the bathtub by hand.

When I cooked for us, I tried not to burn any food. Most of the food was edible. At least no one complained. After all, who would tell a sweaty, stressed-out, pig-tailed twelve-year-old that her cooking was bad?

The best part of the summer in Atlantic City was Labor Day weekend. The boardwalk was decorated with fifty festive floats with thousands of flowers on them. The fifty contestants for Miss America would each sit on a float and be driven from the end of the boardwalk where the marina was to the center of the boardwalk where the Convention Hall that was hosting the competition was located.

It was quite a sight to behold. Numerous tourists eagerly waited to see all the floats pass by, and each store—including the ice cream parlor, pizzeria, and my grandfather's gift shop—all rented out "The Best Seat in the House" to the potential parade-goers. We took out all of our chairs, folding, standing, soft, hard, wood, metal, owned, or borrowed, and tagged each one for people to rent. Most stores were charging one dollar per seat, while stores closer to the Convention Hall were renting the chairs for a whopping three dollars per seat. From those prime seats, the tourists were able to get a better view of the contestants as they got off the floats and strutted into the hall for the beauty contest.

Grandpa's chairs rented quickly, and it was a very profitable day. There were only ten chairs, but that ten-dollar sale was the average daily income for the gift shop.

Atlantic City, NJ Miss America, Jack Freeman Inc. Postcard

Tina and I had never seen so many beautiful ladies with blue or green eyes before. The beauty pageant contestants' eyelashes were long and their red and blonde hair was unfamiliar to us. They wore lavish and elegant gowns with lace and sashes. They waved so very gracefully at everyone. And they smiled continuously, which made us wonder if their faces might be frozen. It took hours for all fifty floats to pass by.

In the evening, the fireworks started at the Steel Pier. We were in total awe, seeing such magnificent and shining works of art in the sky. We only had seen firecrackers for the Chinese New Year celebration, and they definitely were not this elaborate. We were flabbergasted when we had our own, very first hand-held fireworks—sparklers.

Of course, Grandpa was selling sparklers too. We were the best salespersons for the sparklers. Tina and I waved them all around and laughed as we happily chased each other. Grandpa easily sold them because children of all ages were eager to buy them.

The pageant marked the end of the season, and that meant it was time to pack up and return to New York City. Grandpa stopped by the Acme Redemption Center and cashed in all the stamps we earned from shopping at the Acme store. We got pillows, blankets, and a step stool.

We would work in Atlantic City for two more summers until the rent increased and grandfather was too old to drive safely anymore.

"Wow, Nai Nai, you saw horses and beauty queens. Do they still have them now?" Sandy asked.

"No. Sadly, the horses were retired after people thought they were being abused."

"What's abused?"

"It's when someone is being badly treated," I said.

"Do they still have the floats?"

"No, it costs too much to have fifty floats each year. People were able to buy color televisions in the 70s. They could watch on the TV in their comfortable home the glory, the glamour, the talents, and the beauty of the contestants in both bathing suits and evening gowns. There was no reason to travel to Atlantic City to watch the parade of beauties on flower floats."

"Do we still have Miss America contests now?"

"Yes, but most people do not like beauty contests anymore. They would rather watch movies or television shows. After a while, people stopped coming down to Atlantic City, and the city was losing money. It was very bad for a while for the people who lived there," I said.

"Is it better now?" Sandy asked.

"Yes, it got better. For a while, Atlantic City was doing very well with lots of casinos, buffets, and outlets. There was even a casino with a bowling alley in it, and another one had a Ferris wheel in its lobby. Then, hard times returned. Now, the city is working to attract more business and people again."

"Wow. Do you still go there?"

"No, my dear. Your grandfather and I only go to Atlantic City when we have discounts or coupons. Now that there are no more coupons, we don't go there anymore."

"Do Mommy and Daddy have coupons?"

"Well, like I said, they went to a convention. I am sure they have some coupons. They will have fun, and so will we, while they're away."

Photos of Grandpa and Tina, Summer of 1963

CHAPTER 6

THE EGG

It is a Chinese tradition to sweep the tombs of ancestors and departed loved ones every year. It is called the Qingming. Cemeteries around the world would see Chinese families visiting and burning incense on that day. Surprisingly, the date for Qingming very frequently occurred on the date for Easter. For Qingming, we fold gold nuggets out of joss or incense paper. For Easter, we paint eggs.

"Happy Easter, Nai Nai!"

"Happy Easter, Sandy. Are we ready to paint the eggs?"

"Yes, Nai Nai. Mommie set up everything—the paint, the glitter, and googly eyes. I have stickers, lots and lots of stickers!" Sandy was delighted.

"Wow, look at all these hard-boiled eggs. Are you going to eat them all?" I asked Sandy.

"Well, I will eat one. Most of them will be going to the church tomorrow for the Easter egg hunt."

"Great. The children will really love these beautiful eggs. Let's get started. Do you know why we color the eggs?"

"No, why?"

"Many years ago, Catholics started painting the eggs red to symbolize the blood that Jesus shed for us. The egg itself represented the resurrection."

"Yeah. Jesus came alive on Easter Day," said Sandy.

Sandy started to brush green paint onto a hard-boiled egg and said, "I want to paint a green egg with purple eyes."

"Is it because you like the story *Green Eggs and Ham?*"

"No, I just like the color green."

"Okay. I thought you liked the color pink before," I said.

"Oh, yes. I did. But today, I like green."

"Do you like red?" I asked.

"Sometimes. We have so much red in this house already."

"Red means good luck in Chinese culture."

"I know. You always give me a red envelope for my birthday," said Sandy.

"You may not remember this, but when you were one year old, we had a big birthday party for you. Every guest was given a red egg for good luck."

"Wow, Nai Nai. Did you paint them all?"

"Oh no! That would have killed me. We boiled the eggs in red food dye."

After we painted two dozen eggs in different colors, Sandy started to paste her various stickers and googly eyes on them. She even rolled some in rainbow glitter.

"Let's take a break and rest," I said.

We stepped away from the kitchen table and washed our hands. Then, we sat on the sofa in the living room, resting against the soft pillows.

"You know, my darling Sandy, I want to tell you a story about Great Auntie Tina and her eggs."

"Great. I love the stories you tell me. What happened to Great Aunt Tina and her eggs?"

"Well, let me start from the beginning, when she was born."

Sandy leaned back and cuddled up to me as I embraced her in my arms. She was ready to hear the story.

In 1953, my sister, Tina, was born in Shanghai prematurely at twenty-eight weeks, weighing approximately 1 kg. (2.2 pounds). No one expected her to live. The other nurses suggested to Mama that she shut off the incubator and let Tina go in peace, especially since Mama already had a son, Kyle, and a daughter, me. That was plenty already, they said. But Mama could not do that. So, she used an eye dropper to feed tiny Tina until she was healthy enough to leave the hospital and was able to feed from a wet nurse.

Due to her small size and weak immune system, Tina was frequently ill with fevers and infections. She was very fragile and almost died when she contracted meningitis. It was very fortunate that Mama was an exemplary head nurse in the hospital. She was well respected and was able to get the necessary antibiotics and medical attention for Tina.

At the time, all the food and clothing in Shanghai was rationed. Nutritious foods like eggs required medical authorization. Tina's very weak condition warranted a prescription for one egg per month. The egg was her medical supplement, and only Tina was allowed to eat that egg.

In 1959, when Tina was six years old, she had lost a lot of weight after contracting chickenpox. At the time, Tina was only thirty inches tall and weighed twenty pounds. It was then that Mama applied for a short visit to Hong Kong to get a medical consultation for her. She included me as well, stating that I also had kidney problems. Due to her extraordinary work record, the hospital never questioned her request and agreed to let her travel to Hong Kong with us. They were certain that my mama would return since her firstborn son, Kyle, and her youngest daughter, Jade, remained in Shanghai with my father.

In the summer of 1959, Mama took Tina and me on a life-changing, tumultuous journey to get to Hong Kong. Looking back, it was God's will to use the most unlikely, smallest, and sickliest child to be the greatest impetus that spurred phenomenal change in our family. Tina's illness prompted our journey to leave China. And her fever stopped us from getting on the boat that crashed on the rocks and sank. She saved our lives and prevented us from drowning that day in Macau.

When we finally settled in the refugee area of Kowloon, Hong Kong, Mama telegraphed her parents—my grandparents— in New York, who immediately sent her a monthly stipend to support us. Part of the money was sent back to Shanghai to my father. Mama soon became the buyer for my grandfather's gift shop in NY, which sold the Chinese arts and crafts I told you about. Mama visited factories and warehouses to order merchandise to be shipped to and sold in New York.

With that stipend, Mama could afford to buy more nutritious foods for the three of us to eat. We rented one room in an apartment owned by a relative and shared the kitchen and bathroom with other boarders. We were all transient sojourners from China, hoping to migrate to other countries like Spain, Brazil, and America.

Tina's health improved during the three years we stayed in Hong Kong. But Mama insisted that Tina continue to eat one egg per week. Mama would actually buy two eggs and gave the yolks to Tina to eat while Mama and I would eat the egg whites. The yolk had all the nutrients that were good for Tina. Mama would buy one can of condensed milk weekly and added boiling water to make two cups of warm milk for Tina and me.

Life was simple but good. The only difficult time we had was during the severe drought in Hong Kong that lasted two years. For just two hours each day, residents were allowed to collect water using their own vessels, like pots, pans, cups, bowls, and basins. Tina, Mama, and I would wait in line to get water, each holding a bowl and a pot. The water was used for cooking, cleaning, and bathing. Tina and I had small hands and could only collect water with small bottles and bowls.

Mama had a friend we called Auntie Betty, who lived in New York. She visited Hong Kong once during the drought. She invited Mama and us to her expensive hotel room to take a bath. That was the nicest bath the three of us had in two years.

Auntie Betty also knew a dentist in White Plains, New York. That dentist was kind and willing to sponsor Mama as a nurse in his office. In 1962, nurses were in high demand and Mama was approved for a work visa to come to New York and bring us with her. That's how we finally came to America! We soon lived with Grandma and Grandpa there.

In America, better foods were available in larger quantities. But Mama still insisted that Tina continue to eat two egg yolks a week, while I eat the egg whites. After all, Tina was still very small and fragile. One day, my grandma noticed the disparity. After I explained why Mama always gave the yolk to Tina, Grandma immediately boiled more eggs and insisted that I eat a whole egg!

I had never tasted an egg yolk until then. It was delicious and rewarding, knowing that I, too, was eating something good for my health.

Like all siblings, Tina and I often quarreled. If I was losing the argument, I would bring up the fact that Mama always loved Tina more because she was the only one who was allowed to eat the egg yolks.

The story of the egg became comic relief during many family occasions over the years. Tina became very tired of hearing that she gobbled up all the eggs at every holiday or family gathering. If anyone even mentioned an egg, we would start arguing about who Mama loved best. Even after consuming thousands of eggs in her lifetime, Tina remained petite. Even as an adult, she was still only four foot ten inches tall and weighed eighty pounds.

In 1979, my brother and sister, Kyle and Jade, were finally sponsored by my mom to come to America, after China was recognized and trade was established with the western world. They were very happy to be here, and it was wonderful to see them again, after seventeen years apart.

Like us, they were soon able to eat eggs of all kinds, like preserved or salted, duck, quail, or chicken, and even the so-called thousand-year-old fermented black eggs. Everyone loved to eat Mama's famous dish, braised pork butt with braised eggs. Mama made sure that there was at least one egg for each person and sometimes more.

That first Christmas in 1979 when we were all reunited was especially festive. It was the first Christmas that Kyle and Jade had ever experienced. They were thrilled to receive beautiful, colorful new clothing, instead of the drab uniforms they had to wear in China. Jade was grateful to have soft woolen socks which covered her badly scarred feet from worms and insects biting her in the rice field.

Tina and I also exchanged gifts.

"Sit down when you open my present!" commanded Tina.

I obeyed and sat down next to Mama. Under the wrapping paper was a six-inch box. I carefully opened it and found another four-inch box inside. Everyone looked on with curiosity.

I opened the second box and there was an even smaller box inside. Everyone laughed, believing Tina was trying to trick me.

"What did you buy me? Why waste so many boxes?" I asked Tina, slightly annoyed.

"Just open it. You will like it," she said.

"I hope it is not expensive. I only spent ten dollars for your gift," I joked.

"Just open it."

I opened the box and found a smaller, square, 2" x 2" velvet box.

"Oh no, you bought me jewelry? That is too expensive. Take it back," I said. "I don't need jewelry!"

"Just shut up and *open the box*!" Tina shouted.

"All right, all right. Don't get upset. It is Christmas, after all," I said. Everyone leaned in closer to see what was in the velvet box.

Carefully and slowly, I opened it and gasped—and I gasped again. Then I burst out laughing so hard that I was coughing and crying at the same time.

"What is it?" Mama asked.

I showed Mama the contents of the velvet box. Mama laughed and gave a thumbs-up to Tina.

"What is it? Show us!" said Kyle and Jade. They were anxiously waiting to see the mystery gift. Tina held it up for all to see.

It was a small, red, enamel egg encrusted with diamond chips and embellished with a network of gold trim. She then lifted the top side of the egg and revealed a pearl ring inside.

"This is a replica of a Russian Fabergé egg. Since you only spent ten dollars for my gift, I only bought you a copy."

Everyone laughed loudly. "This egg represents all the eggs that I ate and you didn't. Now, we are *even*," Tina said, laughing.

"And you two won't ever have to fight over eggs again," said Mama.

She hugged us both. It was the most memorable gift I have ever received. That egg is still in my bedroom next to my family photos.

CHAPTER 7

TEACHER

In the second week of first grade, Sandy came home from school with a very unhappy look. "I don't like my teacher. She is mean and talks funny," Sandy complained as she removed her backpack after school. She plunged her body into the living room sofa. Apparently, her first-grade teacher was not impressed with Sandy and vice versa. "All of my friends are in the other class. They have a nicer teacher."

"How do you know that their teacher is nicer?" I asked.

"The other teacher smiled at me. My teacher didn't."

"Well, that's not a good way to judge a teacher."

"My friends told me that their teacher was nice. I want to be in their class. Can Mommy ask the school to put me in their class?" Sandy wondered.

"I don't think so. Every class has been assigned one set of children. You can't change classes because your teacher didn't smile at you."

"I don't want to go to school tomorrow!" Sandy pouted and ran to her bedroom.

I waited until she was calmer and came out of her room, ready to eat her snack, and chat. "Did you know that Nai Nai was a teacher?"

"You were a teacher?"

"Yes, at first, my students didn't like me either. In fact, I didn't like being a teacher," I told her.

"Why did you teach then?"

"I became a teacher because I waited in a wrong line."

"What?"

"Oh, my darling Sandy, let me tell you about my teaching career," I said softly as I cuddled her in my arms.

My twenty-five-year career in teaching was borne out of a series of seemingly naïve missteps and divine interventions. Over the years, I changed my job many times so I could get more precious time to spend with my children. At first, I was a Therapeutic Dietician in a nursing home, but that required working weekends, holidays, and throughout the summer. So, I transitioned to become a School Lunch Manager, where I was allowed to take unpaid leave during the summer. Unfortunately, that option was quickly revoked when the Board of Education suddenly decided that all lunch managers had to work during summer school.

When I was mandated to work during the summer, I called in sick almost every day. That triggered a medical investigation from the Board of Education. I was told to report for a physical examination by the Board's official physician at the headquarters of the Board of Education.

The Board of Education headquarter was very busy and there were long lines everywhere. I could not find anyone to direct me to where I was supposed to go for my physical. When I finally reached the right medical office, the lines were even longer. While in line, I overheard someone mention that the Board of Education was in desperate need of teachers.

I remembered seeing an "Apply Here" sign in the lobby. It was a line for hiring teachers. The requirements were twenty-four credits in one subject and twelve credits in education courses. Since my major in college was biology and nutrition, I had more than thirty-six credits in science but only four in education. The line to see the physician was so long, I decided to go on the shorter line and apply for a teaching post to keep my summers free, even though the only students I had ever taught were my own well-behaved, inquisitive, and intelligent children, Phoebe and Justin.

On the last Friday of January in 1985, I got a phone call from the Board of Education instructing me to report to work on the following Monday at Wagner High School on Staten Island.

It went without saying that I had no clue as to what to do, how to teach, or even why I was trying to communicate with some unruly, immature, emotionally unstable, and intellectually stupefied creatures called *teenagers*. Their only interest was checking out their new classmates, new teachers, new "stuff" in school—and then checking *out*.

On the third day of my "teaching career," the principal, who knew that I was a neophyte with no teaching credentials or experience, decided to come and observe me. I was not intimidated by his interpretation of how inadequate my lessons were because I had already decided to resign and return to my previous job.

I walked into the principal's office for a post-observation conference and before he could dispense any reprimands or recommendations, I handed him my resignation letter and asked that he release me before my former job was filled. He was dumbfounded.

"No, I will not release you," he said sternly after reading the letter.

"Why not? You know I can't teach."

"A good teacher must also be a good student. You will learn to teach, and I will help you," he said.

Why did he want to help me teach? As it turned out, there was a shortage of math and science teachers, and he needed a body in front of the classroom. No matter how difficult the mentorship would be, he would win on two fronts: 1) he added a much-needed science teacher to his staff, and 2) he achieved a better public image as the principal.

He was known as a bit of a tyrant. Students called him "Mr. Mucho Macho Russo." Helping me was his way of flaunting his "kindness." All the teachers in the school were shocked that he was mentoring me. He was experienced, cunning, and smelled like a rose. I, on the other hand, was a panic-stricken novice sweating like a pig, with severe acne problems.

It was a tumultuously stressful six months. Meeting with him to plan lessons was agonizing, but anticipating his visits to my classroom was even worse. I had to bribe my students with candies and extra credit in exchange for their good behavior and class participation during his visits.

Without a doubt, I made tons of mistakes as a first-time teacher, but I learned a lot in a short period of time. For example, I had no idea that there should be a *Do Now* activity to keep the students busy while I took attendance. There was supposed to be an *Aim* to each day's lesson, which should elicit intrigue or at least some curiosity for the day. I did not know why some students were sleeping in my class. What issues could cause two teenagers to fight in class? Why did some students never come to class? Why did some students come literally empty-handed, with no books or pens? I did not know the answers until I found out later that some of these students had to work to help their families and had no money for school supplies. Some students slept in class because they were tired from working or caring for their younger siblings.

One day, I was writing notes on the blackboard and saw something small and white strike the blackboard. I looked and found that they were tiny pieces of loose-leaf paper rolled into tiny balls. Someone had blown them out of a straw toward the blackboard. There were dozens of these spit balls stuck to the blackboard.

"Who did this?" I yelled. No one answered.

"Okay you win." I put down my chalk and took a deep breath.

"Shut up, you all. The bitch said we won something," shouted one student.

Suddenly, the class was quiet, and everyone was looking at me. What did they win? I thought it was time for a reckoning. I needed to have respect from these students. Otherwise, I would never teach anything to anyone and my hard-earned pay check would be spent on Tylenol and mental therapy.

"I know that you know that I am a new teacher in this school."

"Hell, yeah," responded some students.

"This is a freshman class, and not all of you are freshmen."

Silence.

"You may be aware that senior teachers get better students in their classes. New teachers get students who are repeaters," I said. Some students bowed their heads.

"Many of you may be bored, looking at notes that you've seen before. That's why you thought you didn't need to pay attention. So, you talk, you come unprepared, you come late, and you come to sleep." The whole class was listening. No one was asleep, and no one uttered a single sound.

"Well, if you just want to come here and waste forty minutes, go ahead. But you can do that anywhere. Why bother walking up all those flights of stairs and down a long hall to this old and very hot room with gum-ridden dirty desks and chipped and damaged chairs? This is the last class of the day. Why don't you just cut and go home? Why wait?" Some students actually sat up and listened.

"The way I see it, you have three options."

"What options?" asked the once-asleep student.

"Option one, you can sit or sleep for forty minutes and fail the class. Then you get to go to summer school or repeat this class again next year."

"Huh, screw this," scoffed some students.

"Option two, if you are too tired or have better things to do during the day, you can attend evening school. Day school is already overcrowded."

"Shit, some of us work at night, bitch," said another.

"It is total B.S. if you choose either of those two options. The strangest thing of all, is that this is the last class of the day, and this classroom is on the third floor, and yet you still come here. Why?"

Some younger students were looking at the older students.

"Could it be that you want to be here, even if it's for a few minutes?" I paused and then said loudly, "The third and the best option I see for you is to just *try*."

"What?" some students said incredulously.

"Yes, just *try*. I know biology is hard, and the vocabulary is weird. No one will probably ever use the term endoplasmic reticulum."

The students looked at each other and laughed. They were a little more relaxed and less hostile.

"I am just saying, since you made the effort to come here, why not make the best of it? Why not try to learn something for ten minutes. Maybe, the next day, you might try listening for fifteen minutes."

The students were looking at each other, whispering, "The Chink is nuts."

"I am new at this teaching gig, but I can guarantee you one thing. I don't want to be bored either," I said.

"Yup, me too," a student said.

"I am not going to entertain you with a song and dance. But I know my lessons are not going to be boring and miserable every minute of every day from now till June. That would just kill me."

The class laughed and waited for me to continue.

"So, why don't you try your best to be here, be ready to learn, and I will try my best to make biology fun and easier to understand. We can call endoplasmic reticulum the ER instead."

"Okay. Yeah. You're gonna really pass us if we try, right?" asked a student, flippantly.

"If you really *try*, you will pass this subject on your own," I responded.

Some young students picked up their pencils, and some of the older students shrugged and nodded. And that is how I reined in the repeater students in the last class of the day.

One day, I noticed that the students were excessively chatty and giggly. They were all actively discussing some urgent matter and then quickly turned to me, removed their smirks, and pretended to listen for the lesson.

After five classes of dealing with snickers and sneers, I decided to find out what was so disturbingly intriguing for all of my students. I knew my repeater students were more receptive and less critical of my teaching style. I asked the two girls in the front, who were still laughing, "What is so funny that you two simply cannot focus on the lesson?"

"Well, Miss, it's, umm ..."

"What?"

"It's your shoes, Miss," said one girl softly while giggling.

"What is the matter with my shoes?" I asked angrily.

"Well, Miss, just look at them," another answered with a smirk.

I looked down at my feet and wished and prayed for a gigantic sinkhole to swallow me whole. On my seemingly humongous feet were two of the world's most hideous shoes, one brown and one black! One was flat, and the other had an inch heel. *How can this be?*

Knowing that I had been walking around the school all day with a pair of mismatched and misaligned shoes petrified me. *How can I fix this terrible image? These teenage gawkers will have no respect for me from this day on. I must save myself. I can't have them think that I am senile or colorblind or both.*

I held my head high and took a deep breath. "Well, I don't know why you all think this is so funny," I announced to the class. "This is the *new* style! I have another pair just like this at home!"

The class roared with laughter. Thank God. By making the egregious situation a joke about myself, I was spared any future humiliation from this fiasco. Once again, it was the repeater students who understood that it was okay to make mistakes. I was no different from them, not perfect, and prone to human errors as they were. The best thing of all, to my surprise, was that unmatched shoes became quite trending in the future.

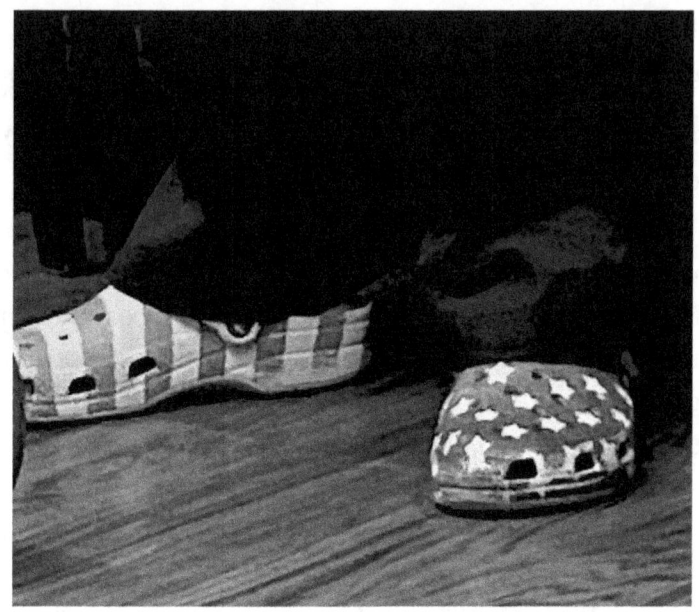

Mismatched Shoes

During the summer of 1986, it was a very happy time for my twelve-year-old Phoebe and five-year-old Justin. They really enjoyed spending two months of fun with me and their cousins. William's family all took advantage of my two months off. His two younger brothers came from Michigan and stayed in our house. His older brother, Dennis, who lived on the next block also sent his three sons to my house whenever we had an outing or dinner. All eight children went together to the amusement parks, movies, and bowling. William's parents loved having barbecues in our backyard throughout the summer. My house was a hotel, diner, and summer camp. It was a very hectic but harmonious summer. One of William's younger brothers decided to send his son from Michigan to stay with us, every summer, for eight summers.

At the end of the summer break, I knew I needed to find another job. Teaching was not my forte. I tried to apply for a bank teller job. The salary was much less than the teaching job.

Then came a phone call from Wagner High School. They wanted me to teach for another year. What? Why? *I can't teach! I don't want to do it again, but I need the money. Oh God, I am headed back to purgatory for another year.*

Knowing that Mr. Russo would return to his megalomaniac self since the mentorship had ended, I prepared myself with better lesson plans and student motivations. Realizing that teaching might be my ultimate career, I took classes in education and methods of teaching. I also needed educational courses to be licensed.

I learned that the students needed me as a source of support, information, academics, and also leadership. I learned to project my voice clearly and loudly to signify confidence and control. I was not afraid to reprimand the lazy and unruly, call the parents of the chronically absent, or even send the nefarious monsters to the school's dean.

The lessons became more interesting. The *Do Now* activity was no longer busy work. Together with a pivotal *Aim*, students were curious and provided actual responses. Many models and experiments were used to enlighten the essence of the topic and provoke cognitive thinking.

One of the lessons that intrigued my students was when I poured a flask of blue solution into a flask of the pink solution, resulting in a clear solution. What happened? Was it a magic trick? No, neutralization of an acid by a base happened, and it was a great teaching moment.

The students also learned about the power of invisible air pressure when I turned a glass filled with water covered only by an index card upside down and not a drop of water dripped out.

I left the glass hanging from the ring stand for days. Still no water dripped out. The students were amazed and fascinated by the strength of air pushing upward.

Generally, it was forbidden for students to eat their experiments, but I allowed them to devour popcorn after they calculated the percent composition of water in a bag of popcorn. A few students even made and ate ice cream in class when I was demonstrating the colligative properties of salt, which lowers the freezing point of water.

My chairman and my colleagues were impressed by my improvement. The principal only visited me once that year and never returned again for observation. Students were no longer bribed. Some were actually happy to be in my class.

The best lesson I gave the students was through a trip to the Liberty State Science Museum in New Jersey. I gave them a list with many questions, for which they had to visit specific parts of the museum to hunt for answers. It was like a scavenger hunt. The bus ride, the gift shop, and the liquid nitrogen and dry ice shows provided by the museum were priceless to them. They were the envy of the students who were not selected to go.

I found more ways to help the students connect what they were learning with the real world by assigning them to read *Brave New World*, by Aldous Huxley. They had to compare and contrast what fantasy in the book had been realized in the modern world. They also learned a lot when I had them read the health section of *Time Magazine*, especially during the HIV/AIDS outbreak.

The school designated one entire day to teach this topic from every academic aspect. When the students reached my class, I let them explain what they had learned. It was truly an effective and illuminating lesson when the students later became enthusiastic teachers for a topic they knew well.

My supervisor assigned me to teach topics like chemistry and physics, for which there was an even greater shortage of licensed teachers, even though I was only licensed to teach biology. It was very daunting, but also fun and enlightening to learn new demonstrations. Indeed, a great teacher must be a lifetime student, eager to continually educate and advance themselves. This pushed me to create more innovative lessons for my students to enjoy and understand.

After teaching three semesters at Wagner High School, I was assigned to another high school. The new principal observed me once and asked me to mentor another new teacher. I was stunned. Was I now considered to be a "good enough" teacher to be a mentor? How did the neophyte become the mentor? It was the highest compliment I had ever received from school administration. However, the best endorsement came from two disgruntled students whose conversation I overheard in the hallway.

"She's insane. She wants to kill us with her shitty demos," one student said.

"She's so unfair. Only her favorite students get to visit museums," said another.

The conversation between the two students continued. I was not surprised by the hatred but was totally shocked that there was envy and jealousy among the students.

"I hate her guts. Tons of homework, impossible tests."

"She never picks me to help her with the demos."

"She never picks me for her trips."

"Did you know some kid stowed away on the bus trip last year?"

"I hope she got into trouble for allowing a student to stow away on her trip."

"Nah. She was fine. But the dumb-ass kid was in real trouble."

"Did you know that her robotic team lost their robot during some competition?"

"What? I bet she was *really* in trouble."

"Nah. Her smarty-pants robotic team built another robot in one day."

"What? I wish I was there to see that."

"Me too. The damn team won an award for it too."

"Oh no! That's the late bell. She is going to close the door."

"Let's go! I wonder what crazy stuff she is doing today."

After hearing my story, Sandy asked, "Nai Nai, I want to build a robot and go to the museums too. Can you take me to the science museum where you took your students?"

"Of course, you will absolutely love it!" I told her enthusiastically.

"Education is the most powerful weapon which you can use to change the world."—*Nelson Mandela*

CHAPTER 8

I Can't Do It

Like many children in elementary school, Sandy also had extracurricular activities after school. Sandy did not like gymnastics or soccer. Instead, she joined a dance and theater class. Driving her every week to learn dancing steps and singing songs was a lot of fun. Everyone was looking forward to the recital in June.

"I can't do the recital. I can't remember all the songs."

"You most definitely will be fine." I said, trying to comfort Sandy.

"No, Nai Nai. I have to sing and dance. I can't do both at the same time."

"You will be fine. Relax. You are just nervous."

"No, no, Nai Nai. I forgot my dance steps in class today."

"Don't worry. There is plenty of time until the recital in June."

"No, Nai Nai. I can't do it." Sandy started to panic and cry.

I hugged Sandy tightly and said softly, "You will be fine. We will practice together and get the steps right."

Sandy was sobbing in my arms. Her skinny body was trembling. I rocked her gently and whispered in her ears, "I was afraid of failing too. But I continued on."

"What were you afraid of?"

"I was going for a test. If I failed, I would lose my job," I said.

"Oh, no. What happened?"

"Let me explain from the beginning."

To become a certified science teacher in 1986, I needed to pass an English test, the National Teacher Examination, and a Laboratory Practical test. The written tests were scheduled in nearby schools. The laboratory test was scheduled at Brooklyn Technical High School.

I lived on Staten Island, and Brooklyn seemed like foreign country to me. It might as well have been Paris, and it felt just as far. On the way to the laboratory test, I was totally lost once I crossed the Manhattan Bridge to Brooklyn. I knew the school was near the bridge. However, I must have missed it, because I found myself driving an extra thirty minutes on the long and busy Flatbush Avenue. *They probably won't let me in to take the test. Should I just go home?* I asked myself.

No, I must not give up so quickly. I was not a quitter. There were no cell phones, GPS, or Google back then. But there were gas stations with maps and attendants who knew the location of the school. It took a few more K-turns and U-turns, but I finally got to my destination. Parking was another impossible feat. After several trips around the school, someone pulled out just in time for my car to squeeze in.

I ran as quickly as possible, huffing and puffing all the way. The school's security guards in the lobby were not impressed that I was lost.

"The test will be over in an hour," one guard said nonchalantly. "They won't let you take it now."

"Well, I am already here. I want to explain myself to the examiner," I said firmly.

"Okay, go to the seventh floor, Room 705."

"Thank you, where is the elevator?" I asked.

"The elevator is not working. You have to walk up."

"What?" I asked, exasperated.

"Yep, they all walked up."

"Okay, where is the ladies' room?" I asked with urgency.

"The restrooms on the second floor are all open," the guard said.

I ran up to the second floor and dashed into a bathroom without looking at the sign on the door. It didn't matter that there were urinals along the wall. I had to pee. My bladder was about to burst from the stress of two hours of driving. My brain was in overdrive. *Why is Brooklyn so far from Staten Island? It must have been God's will. Don't take this test or this job. Who would want to be a science teacher anyway?*

I began to question everything. *Should I climb another five flights? I probably will fail the practical test anyway. I have no idea what laboratory skills a practical exam will be testing. Screw this. I should just go home and not embarrass myself. But I already paid for six hours of babysitting. That's a lot of money. All this time, money, gas, and tolls would be wasted! No, I will climb up, every damned step, every damned floor.*

It wasn't too bad climbing up two flights. I stopped at the landing and breathed deeply. I climbed another two flights, coughing and gasping for air. When I reached the seventh floor, I was bent over, coughing, and panting. I was nearly ninety minutes late.

If I am to be rejected, I need to accept it gracefully. I combed my sweaty hair, put on lipstick, and straightened out my wrinkled dress. There were only two people in Room 705. I was too late.

"I am so sorry that I am very late. But I want you to know that I was *truly very* lost, couldn't find parking, had to pee, and then had to climb up seven flights." I let out a deep sigh and asked, "When is the next test?"

One man looked at me and smiled. "Relax, the elevator was out of order and everyone was late, including some of the proctors. You are in luck."

"Really?" I immediately felt relieved.

"There were so many teachers for this exam, we had to group them. They've all had to wait for their turn to go into the lab. You will be the last person in the last group," he said.

"Thank you so much!" I was overjoyed with tears. *Thank you, God. You* do *want me to take this test. You were testing me. No problem, I can do this. I have faith.*

In the laboratory, laid out on the black slate tables were Bunsen burners, microscopes, test tube racks, and various chemical solutions. There was one proctor for every two applicants.

Applicants were asked to use each instrument and every solution to identify specimens or explain the images they saw. I worked my way through, using every instrument except the Bunsen burner. I had used all the chemicals except Benedict's solution. What was I to do with it?

If I have to use the Bunsen burner, I should light it up. Thank God for a full box of matches. I don't remember how to use a striker to light the damn burner. Match after match broke, or blew out, or did not light the burner. The sixth one popped loudly when placed over the burner.

"*Stop! What are you doing?? You are going to kill us all!*" the proctor screamed.

Everyone looked at me. I was so ashamed. There were tears in my eyes. *Oh my God, they all think I am an idiot. I couldn't even light the burner. I should just go home now.* The proctor shut off the gas valve and shook his head. *So, that was the problem. Too much gas! I could have blown up the building.* "Try again," the proctor demanded.

I made it this far. I can do this. How hard can it be to light a match, then light a burner? Come on, think positively. If they can do it, you can do it. Think hard: How do you light a Bunsen burner?

Calmly, I lit a match and tried to light the burner. No flame. *Oh God, I can't believe that I will fail this godforsaken test because I can't light a burner.* The proctor shook his head again and turned on the gas valve. *Aha, now there was not enough gas! The gas was the problem, not me.*

Finally, I struck another match, the burner was on, and the flame was blue! Now, what to do with Benedict's solution? What was it used for? From the corner of my eye, I saw other tables had a blue or orange solution in a test tube heating in a beaker.

What orange solution? I searched and inspected everything again. Nothing was orange. Every solution was clear except for the blue Benedict's test solution. Aha! *There you are, my sweet glucose! You are the substance to be tested with the blue Benedict's solution!* At last, I was so proud of myself when the blue Benedict's solution turned orange in the presence of glucose and heat.

I was tempted so many times to turn back and quit. Had it not been for that inner voice pushing me onward, I would never have become a licensed and appointed science teacher. Positive thinking with determination can make possible what seemed impossible before.

"Wow, Nai Nai, that was very scary!" said Sandy.

"Yes, it was. But the point is that I did not give up. You should not give up either. We will practice the steps, and you will dance beautifully and perfectly at the recital."

In retrospect, the proctor might have passed me because the Board of Education was very desperate for science teachers. Completing that Laboratory Practical test, despite many obstacles, definitely changed my life. I taught science in New York City high schools for twenty-five years. I told my students about this experience every year when I taught them how to light a Bunsen burner with care, perseverance, and only a small amount of gas.

"Never let the fear of striking out keep you from playing the game." *—Babe Ruth*

CHAPTER 9

SNOW STORM

Winter in New York usually has many blizzards with twenty-inch-thick snow drifts.

Recently, as global warming became more apparent, people were becoming both happy and sad that snow had not fallen on the busy Big Apple for three winters. Students were disappointed because the schools did not close due to the lack of snow storms. Skiers had to drive further north to find authentic fluffy white powder instead of the man-made kind. But most people enjoyed the warm and sunny winter days. In February 2024, a sudden and much welcomed snowfall stormed into New York.

"Nai Nai, there is no school today. Yay!"

"There are only six inches of snow outside," I told Sandy.

"Let's go out and make a snowman!" she shouted with joy.

"I don't think there is enough snow for that. But we will try to make a tiny one."

Sandy and I bundled up and went outside to pile up snow together. It was the first snow of the year, and it was soft and fluffy, light and white. The fresh air was clean and cool.

"Take a deep breath. Enjoy this wonderful fresh air," I said.

Sandy took a deep breath and said, "Okay, let's go make a snowman." She dashed across the front lawn, trying to scoop up snow with her thick gloves, giggling all the way.

"You are so lucky to be able to play in the snow. Many people had to walk to work in the snow or just work in the bitter cold snow."

Sandy fell to the snow and shuffled her arms and legs back and forth to make a snow angel.

I sat down in the snow and tried to collect and roll some snow into a small ball. Sandy sat up and did the same thing, ending up with even smaller balls.

"In the twenty-five years that I worked for the Board of Education, we never had a snow day. Schools were never closed."

"Why not?" Sandy asked.

"Because the public schools provide free breakfast and lunch to those students who need them."

"Don't they want to stay home?"

"No. Usually, their parents are working. There is very little food at home. Some children don't even have a home," I told her.

"Where do they live then?"

"Some children have to live in a shelter where lots of strangers live together."

"What's a shelter?"

"When people do not have a place to live, some live on the street and some lucky ones can live in a shelter, sharing a big house with other families," I said.

"That's terrible," Sandy said. "Do they have their own rooms?"

"No, sweetheart. They have canvas cots for beds. They share the bathrooms. Usually, there is very little food."

"Oh gosh, that's awful!"

"Yes, indeed. Many children are less fortunate than you. You are very lucky to have your own bedroom, lots of toys, and plenty of food."

"Mommy said we should donate clothing and toys. Do they go to the shelters for the poor children?" Sandy said.

"Sometimes. Many people donate money and toys all year round to help the less fortunate people."

Sandy suddenly stood up and said, "Let's go inside."

"Why? We didn't make the snowman yet," I said.

"It's okay. I want to look for toys to give to the poor children," Sandy said.

"That's very kind of you. I am so proud of you."

She quickly rushed toward the house. After she searched her room for toys that she no longer played with, she put them by my side and said, "Let's give these toys to the kids in the shelter."

"Very good. The children will love these toys," I said. "Look at them all: Barbie, dinosaurs, and so many stuffed animals. But I don't think stuffed animals will be accepted."

"Why?" Sandy was concerned.

"Since COVID, stuffed animals and pillows are considered dangerous," I said.

"Dangerous?"

"Yes, they may carry germs."

"Okay. Let me look for something else," said Sandy.

While she was upstairs rummaging through her toy chest, the doorbell rang. I opened the door and saw two teenage boys with shovels in their hands.

"Hi, miss. Do you want us to shovel your walkway?"

"Sure, how much?" I asked.

"Just twenty dollars," replied one of the boys.

"What? Are you going to shovel all the sidewalk around the house?"

"Oh, you have a corner house. That's going to be thirty dollars then."

I was shocked, but then I thought about it and sighed, "Okay, you can do it." The two teens started to shovel the steps and worked their way down to the sidewalk.

Normally, my son, Justin, would use his snow blower to clear the sidewalk, but he was working. I thought about all the times when I could not find anyone to help me shovel snow. It created a daunting nightmare for me that still haunts me every time I see lots of snow. The amount asked by the teenagers seemed exorbitant. However, it will save time and energy for my son. I paid the boys.

In February 1979, there was a winter storm that blanketed New York City with twenty inches of snow. All the businesses were closed. Public transportation came to a halt. Very few people were able to go to work. Thank goodness for Presidents Washington and Lincoln for being born in February. The schools were closed during this snowstorm.

My husband, William, and I always shoveled our own driveway and sidewalk back then. But on that day, we could not find anyone to shovel the snow at William's parents' house, which was one block away. The usual teenagers were very busy making lots of money removing snow for other families. After resting for a while, we finally decided to go shovel the sidewalks for William's parents.

It was then that Mama Tu called and asked her son, William, and me to go over to Dennis' house for dinner. Dennis was the first son, the oldest and most important of her four sons. His family was making dumplings and playing mahjong. William, being the second son, thought we were lucky to be invited.

I was delighted that I did not have to make any dinner. Shoveling the snow in front of our house had already exhausted all my energy. We brought our shovels and walked slowly and carefully to the next block. My four-year-old daughter Phoebe was looking forward to playing with her cousins, Max and Jeremy, sons of Dennis.

Mama and Papa Tu had a two-family house with two driveways and a sixty-foot front yard. William and I got to work, and it took another two hours for us to finish shoveling all the snow. Back then, we were in our early thirties, and we were both strong and healthy. The slight back pain and muscle aches we had were easily relieved with Tylenol.

When we arrived at Dennis' house, we saw that his sidewalks and driveway were still full of snow.

"Why hasn't Dennis shoveled around his own home?" asked William.

"Why doesn't Dennis shovel your parent's house?" I asked in an irritated voice.

"He is the first born. He doesn't have to do anything. I am number two. I do everything," William responded calmly.

"Do you think that is fair? I don't think so." I reminded him of how everyone is equal in America.

"Fair or not, that's how we were raised. There are no equal rights in the Chinese tradition. Can't change that now."

"But your two younger brothers should pay for snow shoveling service since they are never here to shovel snow."

"They've got plenty more snow to shovel in Michigan," he said.

"It's still not fair that we are doing all the work. What if you or I get sick? Who will they call?"

"Stop complaining. It is what it is. The first son gets everything done for him," said William, visibly irritated.

We went inside Dennis' split-level style house and sat on the steps of the lower level to take off our wet boots and coats. William yelled to his parents that the snow was now removed from their sidewalks and driveways. Mama Tu thanked him.

It was then that Regina, Dennis' wife, came running out of the kitchen. "Did you bring any food?" she asked us, sounding aggravated.

"Aren't you guys making dumplings?" I asked.

"Well, I can't make that many dumplings all by myself."

"Well, aren't your mom and husband helping you?"

"What help? They are playing mahjong with Mom and Dad Tu," she said as she stomped off into the kitchen.

"Don't take off your boots!" shouted Mama Tu.

"Why?" asked William.

"You should go out and shovel the snow for your brother's house."

"Why? He can do it himself," William resisted.

"No, he can't. He is playing mahjong with us," said Mama Tu.

"Well, let William play and then have Dennis go out to shovel," I yelled loudly as I went upstairs without my boots. No one responded to my suggestion.

In the living room, Mom, Dad, Dennis, and Regina's mom were sitting around the square mahjong table. They did not get up from their seats to greet William or me. They were very happy and enjoyed shuffling the tiles for the mahjong game that was traditionally called the "Battle Within Four Gates" because the mahjong tiles were arranged like a square fort.

William and I sat on the sofa to rest. Meanwhile, Dennis' firstborn son, seven-year-old Max, was chasing my daughter, four-year-old Phoebe, and forcibly snatched her favorite small green pillow. The pillow provided security and comfort for Phoebe. She was crying while trying to get it back. Dennis' second son, six-year-old Jeremy, was following Phoebe, but was unable to engage Max, who was bigger and meaner in his gestures.

"Max, give the pillow back to Phoebe," I ordered sternly.

"No, I want it."

"You don't want it. You just want to tease Phoebe."

"Don't yell at Max," Mama Tu protested. "He is just playing. His father was just like that when he was young, always taking things from other kids," she laughed.

The first grandson, Max, was the crown jewel. No one could say anything negative about him. No discipline was needed. Max was seen as perfect in every way, even when he bullied his younger brother, Jeremy. It was acceptable because his father, Dennis, was also a rambunctious bully when he was young.

I got up from the sofa, took the pillow from Max, and gave it back to my precious Phoebe. Max ran to his room, pouting and pounding the floor. Phoebe and Jeremy continued to play with Jeremy's trucks.

Regina was the only one in the kitchen chopping the chives and cabbages. She was very angry that she had to prepare dinner for seven adults and three children. The loud clanking of pots and pans was her way of protesting and venting.

I looked at William with a deep sigh. We had been duped. The dinner invitation was Mama Tu's way of getting help for Dennis, either with us making dumplings or shoveling his snow. She wanted her first born to sit and play mahjong with her while we did all the work.

William took a deep breath, "I'd rather shovel the snow. I don't want to make dumplings with that sour puss face Regina, do you? Come on, we have already shoveled some of the sidewalk, but we are not shoveling the driveway."

William and I went back out into the bitter cold. We spent another hour clearing the sidewalks. After shoveling nearly two feet of snow from the sidewalks of three houses, we came back inside and collapsed on Dennis' sofa. We did not say a word, and not one word of gratitude was uttered by anyone.

"Well, are you going to help me wrap the dumplings?" Regina asked, coming out of the kitchen in a huff.

William and I looked at each other and shook our heads. We had been tricked again. A very arduous and relentless day was becoming a dreadful and unmerciful night. Regina had prepared the dough and was rolling out thin wrappers ready for fillings.

It was like a three-ring circus in the house. In the quiet kitchen were three very infuriated and exhausted adults, wrapping dumplings without speaking to each other. In the living room were four joyous adults, laughing and talking about all their winning hands. In the bedrooms were three children, running, laughing, screaming, and fighting over one toy or another.

William and I ate very little, worn out by an exhaustion we couldn't describe and body aches we couldn't quite define. After a while, Phoebe said she hated Max and wanted to go back to our house. We left shortly after the dumplings were served. When we got home, we only had enough energy to take very quick showers and then crumple into bed.

William was willing to accept his fate and duty of being the second son, even though he knew it was wrong for his parents to favor Dennis over everyone else. But he never complained about doing the extra chores while Dennis sat and chatted with his parents.

All of Dennis' younger brothers knew about the unfair and preferential treatment Dennis received. It had been going on for years. For example, Dennis was afforded the luxury of taking a flight to attend college away from home in Oklahoma. The number three son had to endure a forty-two-hour ride on a Greyhound bus to attend college in Kansas. But again, no one complained or voiced any objections because Dennis had saved Mama Tu from a lifetime of shame and embarrassment.

You see, Mama and Papa Tu's marriage started on very shaky ground. Mama Tu had many insecurities before and during their marriage about her appearance and her ability to perform the typical wifely duties expected of her. She was considered to be ugly because she had a cleft palate. She always walked with her head lowered and her back arched forward, trying to hide her face.

Mama Tu considered her first born son to be her savior. She often told us that she feared her husband would reject her and disavow the marriage if she could not produce a son for him. In the old tradition, men could have many wives and could rescind or disclaim their marriage anytime and send the wife back to her family.

She was nineteen when she wed, already considered old for a bride. Papa Tu was three years younger, just sixteen years old, when he wed Mama Tu. He had been suffering from an eye illness for a few years at that time, with his vision deteriorating. Tradition and superstition stated that a happy event such as a wedding would bring good fortune to those who were suffering from misfortune, like his eye disease. Hence, the marriage was quickly arranged.

Back in those days, marriages were arranged by family members, with the future spouses not even meeting directly until the wedding day. However, Papa Tu was able to sneak a peek at the woman he would wed before the big day and have some say in who his future spouse would be. He went to a garden where two sisters were waiting. He selected the younger and prettier girl, not the older girl who was trying to hide her cleft palate by lowering her face.

On the day of the wedding, as per tradition, the bride's face was covered by a red silk scarf throughout the wedding ceremony. He only saw her face when he lifted her red veil in their wedding chamber. When he did, he was shocked and devastated, and stepped back a few steps. The woman he had just committed his life to was the older girl with the cleft palate.

He immediately wanted to disavow the marriage. Mama Tu was trembling and started to cry. She apologized for the switch and tried to explain her situation. Her parents thought that she would never be able to marry anyone due to her facial defect. Therefore, they had to marry her off first and were willing to give the groom's family lots of jewelry, silk, and gold as the dowry.

Papa Tu was educated and was well versed in the Confucian doctrine of never breaking a promise or a vow. He took some deep breaths and sighed a few times. He was pondering his decision and his fate. He saw a helpless woman without any future, crying for his mercy. *What would be the fair thing to do?* He wondered.

"I guess it really doesn't matter much. I might be blind soon," he said sadly and quietly.

"What? You are going to be blind?" she asked.

"My vision is worsening. That's why my parents wanted me to get married now. I want to be able to see beauty before I can't see at all."

"If you go blind, I will take care of you," she said.

"You wouldn't mind taking care of a blind man forever?"

"No. I hope you won't mind my ugly face." She lowered her head with shame. She then paused and lifted her head. "But, I don't think that I am that ugly. I promise you, in the dark, you will like me. You won't see my lips."

The marriage was saved, and Papa Tu's vision improved. He did not go blind. He was able to see by wearing glasses. Mama Tu would eventually get her cleft lip and palate repaired when the family moved to Taiwan in the 1950s.

Mama Tu worried again about her status as a wife when her first child was a girl. In the old tradition, sons were favored and men could rescind their marriage or secure a second spouse if the first wife did not produce an heir. Fortunately, Mama and Papa Tu's daughter was born healthy and beautiful, and adored by everyone.

In the summer of 1941, Papa Tu's teenage brother took his four-year-old niece to the nearby park. The young girl was very thirsty when they got home and immediately drank a glass of water that was sitting on the kitchen table.

Mama Tu came to greet them and noticed that the glass was empty. She immediately told Papa Tu that it was not water. She was making noodles and needed some alkaline salt water, which adds flavor and texture to the noodle. Their daughter was moaning and vomiting, and they asked their rickshaw driver to take them to the hospital as fast as he could. It was thirty minutes away.

When they reached the hospital, their daughter was convulsing and foaming at the mouth. There was nothing the doctors could do to save her. The alkaline salt water was not made of baking soda; it was made of lye for faster results. Their daughter's intestines were damaged beyond repair, and she died in excruciating pain.

Mama Tu mourned in anguish for weeks. She blamed herself for her carelessness. The fear of being sent home by her husband also plagued and tormented her. She was considering drinking lye and killing herself to end it all.

Papa Tu was equally agonized and mortified by the sudden loss of his beloved daughter. He was also very worried that his wife would commit suicide. His teenage brother, who had been living with them after their parents passed, was not sympathetic at all. He was constantly saying, "She killed your daughter. Send her home. You can get a much prettier wife who will give you a son."

Both Mama and Papa Tu could not believe the callous and disheartening comments made by the younger brother, who had been living with them since he was ten years old. His negative comments did not pull the already distraught couple apart—in fact, it brought them closer together and cemented their relationship.

"Thank you, God of Heaven and Earth!" Mama Tu said. She was relieved to learn she was not being replaced.

One year later, Dennis was born, and her marital status became permanently secure. This is why she always considered Dennis her savior. He would always be her favorite. Years later, she was blessed with three more sons.

I empathize with Mama Tu. Life was not easy for a woman living in the early 1900s. Mama Tu did not receive an education past early grade school. She was lucky not to have had her feet bound. Her Manchurian ancestors did not practice that tortuous tradition. Her only skill was learning how to raise silkworms and then selling the cocoons to silk merchants. That is why she believed that her status depended on the whims of her husband. She told me that a wife was the outer garment for the husband. A wife's purpose was to protect the husband and make him look good. If the husband needed or wanted another garment, he could easily throw one away and get a replacement. That explained her insecurity, which I did not like nor accepted.

Instead, I treated Mama Tu just like my own mother. I tried to help both my mothers whenever and however possible. I knew these women were extremely kind and helped raise their younger siblings. Like I said, Mama Tu raised the younger brother of Papa Tu. And my Mama raised her two younger brothers.

However, the two mothers were complete opposites in terms of their personalities. Mama Tu was totally dependent on her husband. In contrast, my Mama was a very independent and intelligent woman. She went to nursing school and was a certified midwife. She even became the head nurse in a Shanghai hospital. She delivered hundreds of babies and was making a very high salary before fleeing Shanghai for Hong Kong and then America.

I wanted to assimilate the good qualities of both mothers. I wanted to be just as independent as Mama, but I also wanted to be patient and tolerant like Mama Tu.

The first few years of my marriage were tolerable. My new sisters and brothers-in-law were courteous, and their children had not yet been spoiled too much. Over the years, though, I turned from being generally agreeable to increasingly resentful for being forced to be the never-appreciated helper for the entire Tu clan.

Whenever the two younger Tu sons visited from Michigan during the holidays and summer, they would stay at my house. My house was "Hotel Tu" for fifteen years because we lived one block away from Papa and Mama Tu. Dennis lived next door to his parents but never took care of such matters as hosting, helping with driving, grocery shopping, or any other chores. He was treated like a prince.

I was the designated driver and servant for the Tu family. I would drive them to their medical appointments and weekly grocery shopping. I hired and paid someone to shovel the snow for my in-laws and also paid for their cleaning lady. Did anyone ever thank me? No.

However, the snowstorm of 1979 was the last straw. That was the rude awakening for William to realize the inequality in how his parents treated us like servants and his firstborn brother Dennis, like the crowned prince. He finally rejected the traditional Chinese culture of favoring the firstborn son. We both agreed that it was totally unacceptable that our manual labor was expected to help make life easier for Dennis. We would never treat our second child, Justin, as any less than our firstborn, Phoebe.

The most unfortunate event happened between 1980 to 2016 when Communist China implemented the One Child Policy to slow down population growth. Every family wanted a son to carry on their name. It created generations of firstborn sons who were also the only child. Countless female babies were killed or abandoned. Only the very cute and adorable baby girls were saved. Many of these firstborn children were over indulged, selfish, and inconsiderate. They never had siblings, cousins, aunts or uncles. Many never learned to share or compromise. It created serious social-economic problems for the future. Twenty years later, the population of males was much greater than that of females. The demand for beautiful women to wed became very problematic. Some beautiful women would demand an exorbitant dowry for marriage, like the purchase of an apartment. This was a far cry from arranged marriages of days gone by, where the women had no rights and no social standing.

Photo of William's Parents

CHAPTER 10

FOOD FOR THE FESTIVALS

Sandy likes to play with dough and make cupcakes. She loves to sprinkle colorful dried fruit pieces onto the cupcakes so they look like they are covered with confetti. Sometimes, she makes a dozen cupcakes and eats half of them all by herself.

"Nai Nai, can we make Frutti Fetti cupcakes today?"

"Sure, honey. You make such colorful and delicious cupcakes. Everyone loves them," I said.

I opened a box of cupcake mix and put little pouches of dried fruits and sprinkles—the "fetti," as she calls it—on the table. All we needed were some eggs and milk. Sandy mixed the batter together in a large bowl and then used a big spoon to spoon the batter into the cups of the muffin pan.

While they were baking, she waited patiently, peering into the oven window periodically until they were done. When they were done, she immediately gobbled up two cupcakes, even though they were still hot.

Sandy's specialties also included making scrambled eggs and pancakes. She loved eating three little pancakes that she arranged to look like Mickey Mouse. Sometimes, she would add green or blue food coloring to her scrambled eggs. She was so creative at the ripe old age of eight.

As she showed more interest in eating different kinds of foods, I decided to introduce her to foods that Chinese people traditionally make during our holidays like zongzi, moon cake, and tofu balls.

"Darling Sandy, would you like to learn how to make zongzi?"

"What's that?" she asked.

"It's a special food that we eat during the Dragon Boat Festival."

"What's a Dragon Boat Festival?"

"Well, let me tell you a story about a noble advisor to the Chinese emperor from a long, long time ago," I said.

"Qu Yuan was his name. He advised his emperor not to trust a king from the East that Qu Yuan believed would invade and seize the country. The emperor did not believe Qu Yuan and exiled him for treason."

"What's exile? What's treason?"

"Treason means that you are against the government. Exile means you are sent away, far, far away from your country," I explained to her.

"Where did Qu Yuan go?" Sandy asked.

"He was sent to a small fishing village in the southern part of China."

Years later, the emperor's country was taken over by the untrustworthy, powerful king from the East. Qu Yuan was very sad that he was unable to prevent this tragedy and threw himself into the Miluo River, in the northern Hunan Province.

The villagers all knew that Qu Yuan was correct, and that the ignorant emperor brought about the fall of the country.

They rushed out to the river in their fishing boats, racing each other in an attempt to recover his body. Unfortunately, Qu Yuan was never found.

The villagers quickly threw rice and other sweet foods into the river, hoping that the fish would eat the food and not the body of Qu Yuan. Every year, on the fifth day of the fifth month of the lunar calendar, the villagers continue to throw sweet rice wrapped in bamboo leaves into the river. Fishing boats race each other in the river in honor and remembrance of Qu Yuan.

The fishing boats were later decorated as dragon boats. The racing of the dragon boats became an annual celebration of the life of Qu Yuan, and the making and eating of the sweet rice wrapped in bamboo leaves has become a traditional holiday food called zongzi (粽子).

Some people like to make the zongzi with sweet rice filled with pork or shrimp, or sweet red beans. Some wrapped the zongzi into rectangles, triangles, or square shapes. My grandma taught us to form them into a pyramid shape.

"How do you do that?" asked Sandy.

"It takes time to prepare the sweet rice fillings. Wrapping it into a shape really depends on how you tie the leaves together," I explained.

"Can we make some?"

I was so delighted that Sandy wanted to learn how to make zongzi. She was now eight years old. Her tiny hands still could not possibly hold the bamboo leaves and fill them with sweet rice. But the fun of washing everything and wrapping the bamboo leaves was a fun and novel activity for her.

Three leaves were needed to wrap one zongzi. Sandy was having trouble holding onto the bamboo leaves with her little hands. She decided to use just one leaf to fill with sweet rice.

Then she folded the bamboo leaf to cover the rice like an envelope and gave it to me to tie it together.

Meanwhile, I put one end of a thick cotton string in my mouth and clenched it with my teeth. Using my right hand, I took the other end of the string and tied it around the zongzi, which was held tightly in my left hand. As the string completely enclosed the zongzi, I released the string from my teeth and tied the two ends together.

My skills were very poor, to say it kindly. The pyramid shape was rarely achieved. My zongzi usually ended up with various vertices, sometimes three or four, and sometimes more. But it was fun making them nonetheless. Sandy and I would laugh at the strange shapes that resulted. The bamboo leaf envelope that Sandy made was tied so tightly that it looked like a small and skinny stick.

After the zongzi was cooked, Sandy was very excited to cut the strings and peel off the bamboo leaves, revealing the red and white Zongzi. We dipped it in sugar and ate it like a dessert. It was yummy.

"Did you know that 2024 is the year of the Dragon?" I asked.

"Will there be dragons at the Dragon Boat Festival this year?"

"I am sure that this year's Dragon Boat Festival will be very special. The boats will probably be very pretty and definitely painted like dragons."

"Can we go see it?" Sandy wondered.

"Of course. We will go see the dragon boat race in Flushing Meadow Corona Lake near the Unisphere in Queens."

"When can we go?"

"In June," I answered.

"Oh, no. That's a long time to wait," she said.

We retired to the living room and rested a while on the comfortable sofa. The zongzi was very filling, being made with sweet rice. We could have easily dozed off. But, I wanted to capture the moment and tell her more about Chinese festivals.

"Time moves very quickly. Before you know it, it will be the Dragon Boat Festival. We love festivals to celebrate our heritage and eat good food with family. We have a lot of festivals. You remember the one we just had in April, right?"

"Humm?" Sandy tried to remember.

"We went to the cemetery to sweep the graves and plant new flowers for my grandmother, your great-great grandmother, and my mother, your great-grandmother."

"Oh, yeah. We were burning paper gold nuggets and lots of paper money," Sandy recalled.

"Yes, that was the Qingming Festival. We paid respect to our ancestors and beloved relatives who died. Then we had a nice and big, delicious dinner to celebrate life."

"Yeah, I love Peking duck. We always order two of them," Sandy rejoiced. "What festival is coming up next?" she asked.

"After the Dragon Boat Festival, we will have the Mid-Autumn Harvest Moon Festival."

"Moon Festival! Oh, yeah. Is that when we eat mooncakes?"

"Yes, those delicious sweet round cakes. And all the family tries to unite for a big dinner."

"Can we make some?"

"No, that is too much work. The professional bakers do a fabulous job. I only buy the sweet ones without egg yolks."

"Is there a story about the mooncakes?"

"Of course. I am so happy that you want to know. Let me tell you all about it."

According to the legend, there was a time in China where ten suns were scorching the earth. Nothing was growing, and the people were dying of heat exhaustion or famine. A master archer named Hou Yi shot down nine suns. People rejoiced and made him the king of the country.

His fame made him greedy, conceited, and corrupt. He demanded more and more contributions from his people. He wanted to live forever and sent out thousands of soldiers in search of an elixir for immortality. Many years later, on the fifteenth day of the eighth month of the year, the elixir was found.

Hou Yi wanted to drink it immediately and live on eternally. His wise and beautiful wife, Chang'e (嫦娥), knew that the people were struggling and that they hated their selfish and brutal king. She did not want the king to drink the elixir and continue to abuse the people for eternity. She snatched the elixir from the king and ran away. The angry king quickly gave chase and attempted to kill her for the elixir. In desperation, she drank the elixir in one big gulp instead of surrendering it to the king. Instantly, she rose and flew to the sky.

The king tried to shoot her down with his arrows. But Chang'e flew to the biggest and roundest moon shining brightly that night. She was able to stay safely there. The country was grateful to Chang'e. The much hated king was killed and peace reigned in the country. Each year, the people remember the sacrifice made by Chang'e by making round cakes that look like the moon and eat them together with their family.

The Heavenly Emperor decided that Chang'e should not spend eternity alone on the moon. He sent her an immortal rabbit to keep her company. Every now and then, you can see a figure of a lady and a little bunny on the moon. Every August 15th of the lunar calendar, families reunite and enjoy a festive dinner while enjoying the brightest and roundest moon of the year.

"Does the rabbit look like my Bunny Boo?"

"Of course. It has floppy ears and fluffy paws. But it is white as snow."

Sandy ran to her room to find her once-pink-now-gray velour bunny with one and a half floppy ears. She returned and wanted to know more stories about Chinese festivals.

"What festival comes after the Autumn Moon Festival? She asked.

"That would be the Spring Festival, celebrating the Chinese New Year."

"Oh, yeah. I love Chinese New Year. I can wear new clothes, new shoes, and get lots of red envelopes," Sandy remembered with glee.

"Cities and villages have lion dances, dragon parades, and lots of firecrackers. We make foods like egg rolls, dumplings, and sweet glutinous rice balls."

I decided to tell her a story about the round tofu balls that my grandmother made during the Chinese New Year.

"Yuck. I hate tofu," Sandy said with a frown.

"But this is not just plain tofu. It's round like a ball and has a little bit of tofu and a lot of other good stuff."

"What kinds of stuff?"

"Pork, shrimp, scallions, and more."

"Is it hard to make like the zongzi?" she asked.

"Well, it was very hard to make when I was young. But now we have machines that help make it easier."

This was the dish that my grandma loved to make during the Chinese New Year and gave away generously to everyone who visited her. Tofu Balls (豆腐圆) is a favorite and popular dish from her home village of Qingtian (青田), China.

When we were young, Tina and I were the designated makers of these one-inch-round, dainty, bite-sized tofu balls. We would stand in the small and hot kitchen for hours to make this laborious food item that everyone enjoyed eating and took home by the dozen.

First, I used a very heavy Chinese cleaver to mince the pork and shrimp. Then, the mushrooms, scallions, and carrots all had to be chopped into very tiny pieces. The food processor had not yet been invented. Grandma added the seasonings and mixed them into the soft tofu. She would cook all the ingredients to be used as the fillings. Then, she left them for Tina and me to roll into miniature balls covered with potato starch.

We pinched off a small amount of the filling into our hands. Then we rolled them into two balls, dipped each in potato starch, cupped one in each palm, and rotated our wrists until they were round and evenly covered with potato starch. Then Grandma would steam them.

Grandma said that our small palms were the perfect size to make the tofu balls, and they looked sumptuous because they were perfectly round. She was so proud that she had two diminutive minions making hundreds of these teeny-weeny-itsy-bitsy tofu balls so that she could give them away as gifts during the holiday.

The tofu balls looked absolutely beautiful. The potato starch created a transparent coating that enclosed the colorful contents. You could see the chopped black mushrooms, pink shrimp, red carrots, green scallions, white tofu, and the browned meat mixture. When Tina and I ate this very colorful and nutritious dish for the first time, they tasted so delicious. After days of rolling them, though, we were so exhausted that we came to dislike the sight and taste of these so-called "New Year Good Fortune Tofu Balls."

In modern days, we would use a small scoop and roll the tofu balls in a large pan of potato starch. All the chopping and mincing would be done by a food processor. But after having made millions of these time-consuming, labor-intensive, little tofu balls, both Tina and I now have no interest in making or eating them.

The mere thought of them brings back unpleasant memories of the long hours we spent standing and the wrist-twisting hard work we did, which could now be qualified as child labor. The soreness in our wrists that pained us for weeks later is still vivid in our minds.

We stopped making them when we moved to Flushing in 1968. During the Lunar New Year, some relatives made some and offered them to Mama. But they really looked and tasted *nothing* like the ones we used to make. These new ones were big, flat, brown, and thick with potato starch. They obviously did not use any food processors or the tiny palms of children.

"Nai Nai, I don't want to make tofu balls."

"Why not?" I asked her.

"It sounds painful. I don't like pain. I don't like tofu."

She ran out of the room and I nodded in agreement. Then, I shook my head sadly, knowing that tofu balls would never be made in this family again.

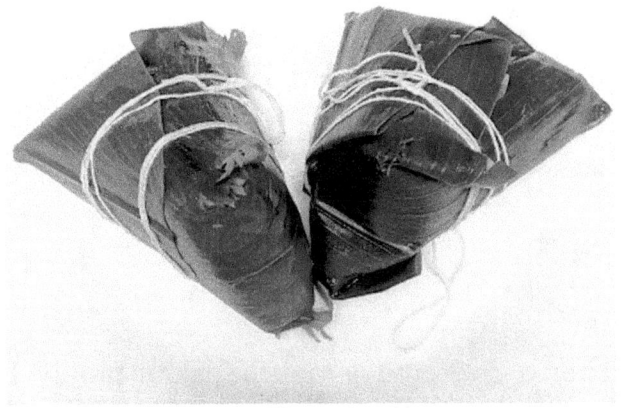

Zhongzi

Mooncake

CHAPTER 11

BEST TURKEY

November is a very busy month for our family. Five people in the family have birthdays, and there are two major holidays, Veterans Day and Thanksgiving. With the addition of Election Day, there were a total of four days with no school. There was lots of cooking and celebrations for the family.

"Happy Birthday, Nai Nai!"

"Thank you, Sandy. Are you glad that the schools are closed on my birthday?"

"Yes. Are you a veteran too?"

"No. But I was born on Veterans Day, a day to celebrate world peace."

"Awesome. My teacher says that World Kindness Day is two days away."

"Perfect! November is such a wonderful month. We can first celebrate peace, then kindness, and then gratitude."

"Are we having turkey this year?" asked Sandy.

"Well, we normally don't eat turkey. The Chinese celebrate holidays with roasted chicken, duck, pig, and seafood like lobster, crab, and fish."

"But all of my friends have turkey for Thanksgiving dinner. I wish we could have turkey just like everyone else."

"Okay, I will roast a turkey this year," I said.

"Thank you, Nai Nai!" Sandy gave me a big hug.

There was one problem. I had never cooked a turkey before and had no idea how to do it. So, I decided to ask my friend Sara if her mom could show me how to prepare the humongous bird. Sara claimed that her mother made the best turkey in the whole neighborhood. All her neighbors and relatives raved about how tender and flavorful the turkey was. They even gladly took leftovers home, if there were any.

I arrived at Sara's house at 7:00 a.m. with a big note pad and pen for my turkey lesson. Sara opened her door with a smile from ear to ear. "You are never going to forget today's high-class cooking lesson!" she boasted. I hugged and thanked her, and we went straight into the kitchen.

On the kitchen counter was a gigantic twenty-pound turkey sitting in a roasting pan. A large tray of assorted herbs, spices, wine, and oil were next to it.

"You are so organized. I have to write down all of these ingredients," I said. I was surprised at how many types of seasonings were needed. Then I looked next to the turkey.

"Wow, that is a lot of stuffing for one bird," I said to Sara.

"Don't forget the onion and celery over there," said Sara, pointing to the vegetables in the sink. "We need them too."

Sara and I washed and cut the vegetables and cleaned the turkey. With intense excitement, I asked, "Okay, what should I do first?" I eagerly held up my pen to jot down everything the recipe needed. "Just tell me how much of what and where to put it," I said.

"Well, this is the best part of the lesson," said Sara, smiling mysteriously. "Roasting a turkey is easy. Seasoning it just right, well, that takes experience," she said confidently. "My mother is the one who seasons and preps the turkey before it goes into the oven," Sara explained.

"Okay, sounds good. Is your mother awake yet? Should we first make her some breakfast?"

"No, she ate her breakfast at 6:00 a.m. She is waiting for us," said Sara.

I looked around and did not see anyone else in the kitchen or living room. "Where is she?"

"Upstairs," Sara replied.

"Is she coming down soon?" I asked.

"No. We are going upstairs to bring her the turkey and the spices."

"What? How are we going to do that?" I was confused by this part of the process.

"She has severe rheumatoid arthritis, so it is very difficult for her to get out of bed. Going up and down the stairs is very painful and impossible for her."

"Oh, no. I am so sorry to hear that. I should not have come to bother her," I said.

"It's no bother. Your being here today is actually a good thing," Sara said, smiling.

"If I had known that she was in pain, I never would have come. She must hate me for bothering her to teach me how to cook a turkey."

"Nonsense," said Sara. "Your request for her recipe is more precious than gold to her. You made her feel important, useful, and very smart. Come, let's go upstairs and dress the bird. She's waiting for you."

I put down my writing utensils and offered to carry the roasting pan with the turkey. Sara shook her head and put the roasting pan onto a wheelchair—yes, a wheelchair. I was getting more confused by the minute—a little baffled, to be honest.

Sara carefully pushed the wheelchair to the staircase in the living room. She pushed a button on the wall to bring the stairlift to the bottom of the steps. She lifted the guard rail and put the roasting pan with the turkey onto the chair. She pushed the button again, and slowly, the turkey ascended with its wings in the air. I had never seen a turkey riding an escalator.

Both Sara and I walked up to the second floor to meet the turkey. It was then lifted onto a service cart, which was already waiting on the landing. Sara pushed the service cart into the master bedroom. Mrs. Green was sitting up in her hospital bed, smiling and waving us in. I felt so guilty about asking a fragile, skinny, white-haired elder to prepare a turkey. I apologized again and again.

Mrs. Green was very happy to see us. She said in a soft and raspy voice, "I can't wait to show you how I dress my bird." She looked around and asked, "Where are my seasonings?"

Sara rushed down the stairs and quickly placed the vegetables and the tray of seasonings on the stairlift and sent them upward. With all the ingredients at hand, Mrs. Green used her tiny wrinkled and shaking right hand and poured a pinch of this, a splash of that, a spoon of "what's its name" and sprinkled some "whatchamacallit" on the huge bird. She then stuffed the turkey with onions and celery and massaged it with lots of crushed garlic, rosemary, orange peel, and oil. "Don't forget to baste it with orange juice," she reminded Sara as we left the room.

The very shiny and super oily turkey was now ready for its trip down the stairlift. Once again, the wheelchair was used to roll the turkey to the oven in the kitchen. Once the oven door was shut, Sara and I took a deep breath and burst out laughing.

"You are so right about this being an unforgettable cooking lesson," I said to Sara. "I have never seen a turkey ride an escalator. Thank you very much for this unique opportunity to learn from Mrs. Green."

"Yep! You better believe it. This is definitely a once-in-a-lifetime cooking lesson," she said.

I ended up going home without any notes or recipes. Relying only on my memory, I tried to season my turkey just like Mrs. Green did. But I had less than half of the spices that Mrs. Green used, and the turkey was not kosher, nor was it soaked in a brine solution first to keep it moist during cooking.

Sandy was very impressed by the size of the turkey. "This turkey is seven times larger than you when you were born," I told Sandy. "And look at you now. You are seven times larger than the turkey!" Sandy and I laughed loudly as we rubbed oil and garlic powder all over the turkey.

"Bring me the orange juice from the refrigerator," I told her.

"Why do we need to pour orange juice on the turkey?"

"I am not sure, but Mrs. Green insisted. So, we will pour it over the turkey."

When it was done cooking, the turkey looked golden brown and smelled delicious. The thermometer that was implanted in the thigh popped up. The table was set with knives and forks instead of chopsticks. There was also salad, sweet potatoes, and corn. I did not make other dishes like we usually do on holiday meals. This was an American meal. But I did make a dish of spare ribs and egg rolls for appetizers.

My daughter Phoebe and son Justin and his family all came to our apartment to celebrate Thanksgiving. The spare ribs and egg rolls were quickly consumed. As I carved the turkey with an electric knife, I noticed that the meat was a little dry. I quickly used the drippings from the roasting pan and made a gravy to pour over the meat. I told Sandy that it was not my fault. "It's grandfather's fault!" I exclaimed.

Everyone turned to look at my husband, who looked very confused with deeply furrowed eyebrows.

"What?" my family asked in unison and turned to look at me with wild opened mouths.

"Of course, of course, it's my fault," said William. "Pray tell, my darling, what did I do to your turkey?"

"You didn't do anything to the turkey," I told him calmly.

"Then why is this my fault?" he asked.

"It's your fault, my darling, because I can't cook a turkey if you don't buy me a stairlift!" I said with a broad smile.

After hearing the story of what happened at Sara's house, everyone laughed for a long time and enjoyed the best turkey I ever made.

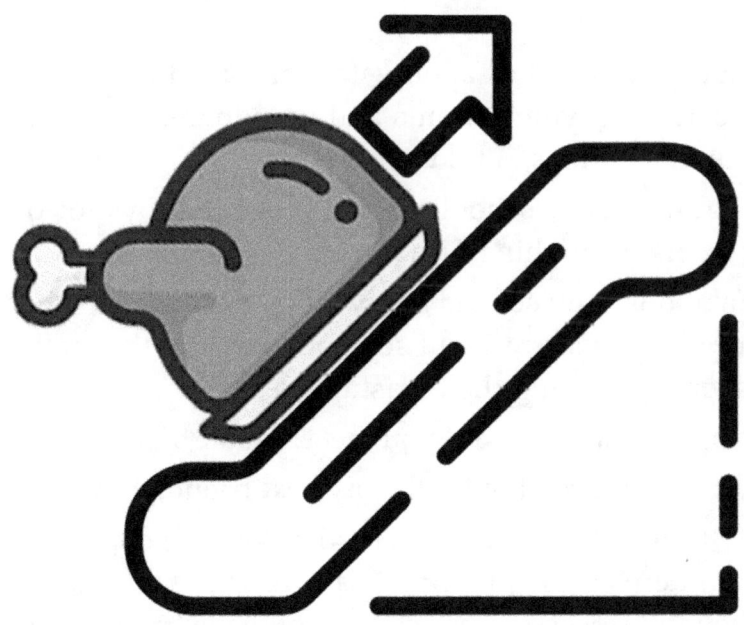

CHAPTER 12

CHRISTMAS FRIEND

Life became very frantic and nonstop rushing after Thanksgiving. Christmas music played on the radio twenty-four hours a day, seven days a week. Cheerful decorations were seen everywhere. Sandy wanted to go shopping for Christmas gifts.

"Not every child or adult gets a gift at Christmas. You are very lucky that your parents and grandparents can afford to buy you nice things," I told her.

"I know. At my school, we are collecting toys for others. I want to find something nice for someone else," Sandy said.

"Fabulous. I am so glad that you are thinking of others. Did I ever tell you a story about someone I met at the mall when I was shopping during the Christmas season?"

"No, Nai Nai. Who did you meet? What happened?"

"Well, she turned out to be my best friend," I said.

My friends have always been the type of people who have similar interests and principles as I do. Those who understand my thought processes, or lack thereof, have become my truest friends. Many of my dearest friends are very familiar with my antics, like calling everyone by the wrong name all the time, and can interpret my awkward wording or unusual behavior without needing clarification. They just understand me and what makes me, *me*. Years ago, in December 1975, I encountered a woman who turned out to be my very own best friend.

It was the hectic season of holiday shopping, wrapping, and giving. I only had time to shop for holiday gifts after one-year-old Phoebe went to sleep and my husband William was at home to watch her. I did not have much time and needed to complete my gift shopping in three hours, or before the stores closed, whichever came first.

The plan was very simple. Having only one income in the household, we must use only what we saved throughout the year in a special Christmas Club savings account. *What was on sale? Who would like the sale item? Who could use it?* Choosing the right gift for each person was very difficult, because I had to take into consideration the person's tastes, but also the percent off, special discounts, and coupons. The coupons, well, they required a magnifying glass and a decoder to figure out.

After three hours, I held three large shopping bags in each arm. I was sweating from wearing a winter coat as I dashed in and out of the aisles looking for signs that read "SALE," "One Day Sale," "60% OFF," and "Buy One, Get One Free!"

But I wouldn't dare to look through the clearance racks. I would be too embarrassed if the recipients decided to return their items and found out. After all that running around, my neck and arms were hurting, so I stepped into an open aisle and took a long, deep breath. In my head, I was double-checking my list of people I had to shop for. Did they give me any kind of hint about what they really wanted? Could I afford it? Where would I find it?

As I looked ahead, I saw in the distance a disheveled woman who was also carrying six bags. She looked familiar. She must have been a friend. *What was her name? She must be just like me, shopping when her kids were asleep,* I thought. The woman's hair was untidy. She was wearing a heavy, gray winter coat, navy blue sweatpants, and a red sweater. Obviously, she had no sense of fashion. Maybe, she was color-blind.

The woman's face looked puzzled and frazzled. She seemed to be looking straight at me. *She must be wondering who I am. Now, think, think, think—who is she?* I panicked as the woman was approaching. *Oh, I must remember her name. What should I say to her? "Hey you? How's the weather?"*

I smiled and waved. The woman smiled and waved. As I approached closer, I saw that the red sweater had several stains and her navy sweatpants had a tear in them. *This poor woman does not have much money or she can't afford decent clothing to wear. But then again, she must have some money; she had so many bags full of stuff. Maybe, she chose to spend her money on others and not for herself. I could definitely relate to that, especially during this holiday season when all the family members needed a gift.*

We, the matriarchs, I said to myself, *must support everyone with loving gifts.* On the other hand, the gifts that we wanted most for ourselves were free and priceless. At that moment, I could really use a grateful hug, a warm embrace, a loving kiss, a kind word or two. That really would have made my day.

At closer range, I could see that the woman undeniably had no time for herself. Her hair was uneven in length. She clearly hadn't been to a hairdresser in months. She did not wear winter boots. Instead, she wore a pair of very old and worn-out sneakers. Her fatigued and exhausted gaze suggested that she was definitely sleep-deprived and could really use some help with the household chores.

I felt like I really understood this woman. I could understand how she did not take care of herself. She must be overworked and overstressed with child care and house chores like me.

As the woman walked closer, I could see the stress and wrinkles on her pale face. The furrows between her thick and untrimmed eyebrows indicated that she really did not know who I was. She shook her head and frowned a little.

Oh no, I can't remember her at all! Oh well, maybe we were just old acquaintances. No need to be concerned. I decided that we would just greet each other and engage in some small talk about the weather.

As the distance between us diminished, I could see more of the woman's face. Not only did she look familiar, she now appeared remarkably similar. *Are we related? Which one of my hundreds of cousins is this woman? What is her name?*

Now up close, I could lean over to touch her. I placed some of the bags on the floor and extended my right hand in an attempt to shake the hand of the woman. A rigid, icy touch brushed my hand, and a glacial chill crawled up my spine. I froze, heart pounding, unsure of what was real. I quickly pulled my hand back and dropped all of my packages. To my surprise, she dropped all of her packages and her jaw.

Oh my God, how can this be? What happened? When did I become so blind or forgetful? Am I touching a ghost? I gasped in disbelief. I was dumbfounded to see how this unrecognizable woman was not just some friend or relative—she was the reflection of the disheveled, disordered and distressed *me* in a silver mirror in the store! *How is that me?*

"Oh my God! That is too funny," Sandy commented.

"Not at the time. It was not funny at all. It was truly horrifying," I said.

That was an earth-shattering, rude awakening for me. I stopped and looked around to make sure no one saw me shaking hands with a mirror. I took a closer look at myself. Indeed, I was wearing worn out clothing that had stains and holes. How and why did I leave my house looking like that? It was time to go home, *now*! It occurred to me that I was not taking care of myself, not sleeping enough, and had paid no attention to my appearance. Why? My one-year-old Phoebe was my only focus. Nothing else mattered to me.

I realized that I really needed to take better care of myself. I must try to get eight hours of sleep on some nights. I would get a very fashionable haircut. Then, I would throw out all of the stained and ripped clothing that I had been wearing. I made a promise to myself: *The New Year would see a new me.*

"Oh Nai Nai, you deserve much more than a haircut. What can I get you for Christmas?" asked Sandy.

"All I need from you is a big hug and a big kiss." Sandy quickly and warmly gifted me.

Sandy also sang me a little song that I had taught her both in Chinese and English words. We always sang this song to each other whenever we wanted to comfort each other. It was amazing to me how she knew to sing this song while hugging me.

Wǒ is I ,
Nǐ is you.
Wǒ ài nǐ is
I Love you.

In retrospect, all of that stress and fuss made me feel frazzled and crazy when I was young. But holding my granddaughter in my shriveled arms now made it all worthwhile. It was extremely rewarding and comforting to know that Sandy knew just when I needed a little tender loving care. The heartwarming inner peace she gifted me was priceless.

CHAPTER 13

HEAVEN AWAITS

Sandy had a pet betta fish named Bee. She enjoyed feeding it every other day. One day, she was devastated and crying profusely when she found out that Bee lay motionless at the bottom of the small fish tank. "Oh, no. Bee is gone. I will never see it again," she said sadly.

"Not true. You will see your fish in heaven," I said, trying to reassure her.

"Is there a fish heaven?"

"There's not one especially for fish. But in heaven, you will see all your loved ones who left earth. Bee will be there too."

Sandy seemed comforted by this.

"Did I tell you that I also had a fish for a pet a few years ago?" I asked her.

"Really, what kind of fish was it?"

"It was a goldfish with two gigantic eyeballs."

"What was its name?"

"I called it Chubby," I said.

"Was it a big fat fish?" Sandy asked.

"Its head was huge with two bulging eyes and its tummy was very round. It looked chubby to me."

"How long did you have the fish?"

"Oh, I think about two or maybe three years."

"That's a long time," Sandy said. "Did it just stop swimming one day, like my Bee?"

"Chubby's round tummy got bigger and bigger. Then it actually started swimming upside down."

"What? How does a fish swim upside down?" Sandy asked.

"I don't know, but the internet said it could've been suffering from some bladder disease."

"Did you take it to the vet?"

"No, my dear. It cost too much money to take a fish to see a veterinarian," I told her.

"What did you do?"

"We watched it, cleaned the tank many times, and added medicine. We just tried to keep Chubby comfortable," I said.

"Did he get better?"

"Well, it continued to swim upside down for a few months. Then, it sank to the bottom of the tank and went to heaven, just like your betta fish."

"Did you cry, too?" asked Sandy.

"Well, I was very sad. I got used to Chubby greeting me every morning when I got up. So, yes, I cried a little."

"Did you bury Chubby?" Sandy seemed very concerned about this.

I couldn't tell her that we flushed Chubby down the toilet, so I changed the subject. "Would you like to bury Bee in the backyard?"

"Yes." I think Sandy was relieved to learn that I, too, had lost a pet.

"You know, every living thing will eventually die, including fish, dogs, cats, and people," I said to Sandy.

"What happens when we die?"

"Well, that's up to what you believe in," I explained vaguely.

"What do you mean?" she wondered.

"Well, some people believe that after we die, we go to heaven, if we are good."

"I am good. I will go to heaven and see Bee."

"Yes, you will. Death is just another part of life. When I go to heaven, I will see my grandmother," I said.

"How did your grandmother die?"

"Do you want me to tell you about your great-great-grandmother?"

"Yes, please," said Sandy.

"Your great-great-grandmother came from a place where fish live and swim in the rice field."

"What? How?" asked Sandy with excitement and curiosity.

Thousands of years ago, the county of Qingtian suffered a great flood. The rice fields were overrun with water and the rice crops died. The farmers were devastated and everyone worried that they would soon die from starvation. People prayed to the heavens and asked for help. Legend has it that one of the eight immortal gods of China, Lu Dongbin (呂洞賓), saved the people of Qingtian.

"How?" asked Sandy.

Lu Dongbin happened to be living in one of the beautiful caves in Qingtian. He heard the prayers of the people and came to the flooded field. He threw into the flooded rice field a handful of sesame seeds and told the farmers to come back in three days.

The farmers waited with anticipation and curiosity. They had heard that Lu Dongbin once threw a few grains of rice into a water well and turned the water into wine. "I hope he doesn't give us wine. We need rice," some of the farmers said.

"What happened in three days?"

"The farmers were shocked to see thousands of fish swimming in the rice field."

"Wow!"

"The people ate plenty of fish until the water level in the rice field receded. Then, the rice crops flourished again so that they could eat rice."

"What happened to the fish?"

"The farmers learned to keep the rice field filled with just the right amount of water, and the fish lived on too."

"That's a wonderful story."

"Farmers in China and other parts of the world are still doing it, it's called Aquaculture. The farmers can grow carp, tilapia, crab, and rice at the same time! In fact, people can go to Qingtian now to tour the rice and fish farming system."

Fish in Rice Field
https://en.wikipedia.org/wiki/Rice-fish_system

"Did your grandma grow fish or rice?"

"Neither. Your great-great-grandma was born into a very wealthy family. She couldn't do any farming."

"Why?"

"Rich families had the feet of their daughters bound when they were toddlers. This way, their tiny feet would prevent them from running away. My grandmother had tiny bound feet and couldn't possibly stand up straight in a muddy, uneven rice paddy. But she ate the fresh fish or the dried preserved fish that lived in the rice paddy. Of course, she ate the rice too. Let me tell you more about your wonderful great-great-grandmother." I continued.

My grandparents had lived on 28th Street and 2nd Avenue in NYC for forty years. In that time, Grandma had become known as the famously generous "Come and Eat" Jing Tai Tai of 28th Street. It was her trademark phrase for any new immigrants moving to NYC from any part of China, especially from her hometown of Qingtian. Everyone knew Jing Tai Tai would welcome and greet newcomers with open arms and warm delicious food, while my grandfather would provide them with new business opportunities. My grandparents were pillars in their community.

In 1981, my grandmother became very ill. It was alarming news to the whole neighborhood. Grandma had been coughing for a week. She was having a hard time breathing. Her friends finally convinced her to walk to the Emergency Room at Bellevue Hospital, which was only one block away. She was admitted immediately.

Many tests were done. Grandma hated getting her blood drawn. After an X-ray, the doctors wanted to do a bronchoscopy to look at her lungs and air passages. Back then, CT and MRI machines had not yet been invented. A bronchoscopy was done with just local anesthesia.

I remembered holding the tiny, trembling hands of Grandma as she sat in a chair with her head tilted back. A nurse was holding her head while two young doctors gently pushed a tiny tube into her mouth and down her trachea.

"Don't worry. She won't feel a thing," one of the doctors said.

"But she is awake and very scared," I told them.

"Tell her to close her eyes and just relax. We will be done in a minute."

"Stop it now," I ordered, concerned. "My grandmother is shaking."

"Almost there. Just tell her to relax. We're almost done."

I panicked when I saw the pale and petrified face of my grandma. One of her small hands was waving *no*, another was holding my hand, squeezing it tightly. Her tiny feet were kicking and shaking too.

"You have to stop now. You are scaring her too much," I told them.

"Okay, we can't find anything anyway," said the disappointed residents. They left the room without any regard for Grandma. The nurse wheeled her back to her hospital bed.

Grandma was shaking and coughing at the same time. Both she and I were crying. It was not a test. It was pure torture. Grandma had never been so scared in her life. I saw a horrified, tiny, elderly woman trembling and felt shamefully helpless.

"I will go yell at the bastards," I said loudly. "They should not have done this procedure while you were awake."

"No, no, just take me home," Grandma said hoarsely.

"But they have not found what caused your cough. You need to stay," I told her.

"No, no. I want to go home."

"The doctors said they must find out what's in your lungs that is making you cough so much."

"Any more tests and I will die," said Grandma. "Nothing is in my lungs. Please just take me home and make me chicken soup." She tried to get out of bed.

Grandma was shaking so much that she fell back onto the bed. I covered her quivering body with a blanket and gently stroked her hands. Grandma was less than five feet tall. Her feet had been bound when she was young, so she always walked slowly for better balance. Her hands were small and delicate, but had a lot of calluses from sewing and pulling threads.

Slowly, Grandma was able to breathe more easily and began to doze off. Either the sedative finally took effect, or she passed out from exhaustion.

Grandpa came to the hospital and told me to go home because my six-year-old daughter Phoebe was waiting for me with William.

"Wow," said Sandy. "That must have been a long time ago."

I laughed and then returned to telling the story. Grandma was much calmer when she saw Grandpa. They both waved for me to leave. That evening, I went to sleep after knowing that Grandma stayed in the hospital and Grandpa was safely at home after his visit comforted her.

Suddenly, I heard a noise and saw Grandma standing next to my bed. I was awake and staring at someone who was not supposed to be there.

"Wait, why are you here?" I asked, shocked. *How did Grandma get into my bedroom? She's supposed to be in the hospital.*

"I want to know why you did not tell me," said Grandma with her arms crossed.

"What didn't I tell you?" I asked. *What is she talking about? How is she here?*

"You did not tell me that you are pregnant," she said.

"What?" I was stunned. *Is this a dream?*

"I know you are going to have a beautiful baby boy."

"What?" I asked again. *What is happening?*

The phone rang loudly. I woke up with a start and turned my head toward the telephone. When I looked back, Grandma was gone.

"Hello?" I said, groggily.

"Is this Anly?" asked the caller.

"Yes, who is this?"

"This is the nurse at Bellevue Hospital. Is Mrs. Jing your grandmother?" she asked.

"Yes, why?" I was starting to worry.

"I am sorry to inform you that your grandmother just passed away."

"What? I think I just saw her. How did she die?"

"Cardiac arrest. So sorry," she said.

"What the heck?! Those residents scared her to death," I yelled.

"What residents? What are you talking about?" The nurse was taken aback.

"Those idiots killed my grandma. I should have taken her home. This is wrong at so many levels."

"Miss Emily, I know that you are upset. Please come to the hospital and talk to the—"

I hung up the phone and looked around the room. I was in bed with William, who was awakened by my screaming.

"Did you see Grandma a moment ago?" I asked him.

"No, what ... Who was that on the phone?" he asked, suddenly awake.

"It was the hospital."

"What did they say?"

"They said Grandma died," I said. "But she was just here! I saw her."

"Where? We were sleeping. You must have been dreaming," said William.

"Oh my God, her ghost came to me just now!"

"Are you sure?" William was surprised.

"Yes, yes. I should have taken her home," I told him.

"What did Grandma say when you saw her?"

I looked at my bewildered husband and said with disbelief, "She said that I'm going to have a baby boy."

I turned to Sandy. "Six months later, my son Justin—your father—was born. Grandma knew!"

"Woah," said Sandy, astonished.

Grandma died at age seventy-two in March 1981, only three days after her admission to Bellevue. All the relatives and friends living on 27th and 28th Streets were shocked. No one could believe what had happened. Many expressed their respectful feelings about her.

"She was so wonderful and generous," said one.

"She was a very good cook," said another.

"She made such beautiful lamp shades."

"No one can do what she did."

"Why did she die so young?"

"She was always healthy, never sick."

"What happened?" asked a neighbor.

"Buddha called her home," answered someone else.

"It was her time to go. It was her fate."

Grandma's funeral was attended by hundreds of people. Most of them were single men, total strangers, who were welcomed by my grandparents to come by their apartment and enjoy a good meal when they needed it most. Grandpa helped some of them find employment.

Buddhist nuns came to the funeral home in Chinatown and chanted prayers for three days. So many flowers and wreaths were delivered that another room was needed to display all of them. Two floral trucks were hired to bring all the flowers to the cemetery.

The procession of her hearse and thirty-five black Town Cars paraded around Chinatown. There was a four-person band marching in front of the hearse—a drummer, two trumpeters, and a flutist played solemn music and *Amazing Grace.*

The people in Chinatown stood still and watched with awe as the funeral procession drove slowly by.

"She must be a celebrity," said one person.

"She must be a noble woman," said another.

"She is very fortunate to have so many relatives."

"Wow, so many people are sending her off. She must be a very good person."

The procession then drove uptown to Grandma's home on 28th Street. The chauffeur opened the door of the hearse, letting Grandma's spirit out to see her old residence. Then all the cars drove to the Cypress Hill Cemetery in Brooklyn, where Grandma was finally laid to rest.

More than one hundred people attended the repast dinner in a Chinatown restaurant called Four Five Six. Everyone praised Grandma and her generosity. Throughout the dinner, sweet memories of Grandma were shared passionately in toasts and speeches. She was well respected, revered, and remembered by so many.

Grandma was a Buddhist. That meant the family had to participate in a forty-nine-day bereavement ritual. During that time, it was believed that the soul of the deceased floats between final death and rebirth. On the 49th day, King Yan, the ruler of the afterlife, would decide if the deceased had done enough good deeds to earn a chance to be reincarnated or should be punished in hell. A truly good person was allowed to live in heaven for all eternity.

The survivors of the deceased were supposed to burn incense and money made of gold and silver colored incense paper during these forty-nine days to provide "funds" to their loved ones as they travel through this portion of the afterlife. Some people even burned paper servants and paper houses so that the spirits could access luxury and comfort in the afterlife.

My mother and my uncles had to attend the temple and chant with the monks seven times, once each week. It was important that Grandma heard their prayers along this forty-nine-day journey, to be reminded of how much she was loved and to keep her motivated as she explored the afterlife.

During the seven weeks, the spirit of the deceased would often return to visit their loved ones. They would travel to the homes of those who helped them to show the latter gratitude. The spirit would also travel to the homes of those who wronged them to collect or forgive a debt.

"Wait, how do they collect the debt?" Sandy suddenly asked.

"Well, they use ghost coins, which is something like Bitcoin, I suppose," I said.

"What coin?"

"You can't really see or touch ghost coins or Bitcoins. They're just numbers in an account."

"Wow. There is a bank in heaven?" asked Sandy.

"Sure. That's why we need to burn paper money every year during the Qingming Festival at the cemetery. That vapor fills the bank account," I explained.

"Can we burn more money next year at Qingming?"

"Yes, and I think I will buy a set of paper mahjong tiles and burn it to send to your great-great-grandma," I said. "She would love that."

Photo of the Gravestone and Paper Mahjong

CHAPTER 14

MAMA WENT HOME

When Sandy was six years old, she was very close to my Mama, who was ninety-three years old at the time. Sandy loved to visit the vegetable garden that Mama had in the back of her house in Flushing, Queens. Mama was growing cucumbers, cherry tomatoes, and eggplants. Sandy loved to pick the tomatoes and cucumbers and eat them like candy.

We would both visit Mama and listen to her tell stories about her time as a midwife, like the baby that she delivered in Shanghai and then had to run three flights upstairs with the newborn in her arms to get the baby into surgery in order to save his life. She broke her leg in the process of running up and down the stairs.

Sandy liked to play with the squeeze balls and pet toys that I gave Mama to strengthen her hands. They both laughed at the fact that neither of them could make the toys squeak. Both had tiny and weak hands. It would take both of them working together to squeeze the slightest sound out of a little rubber bird.

I once bought a stuffed monkey with two very long limbs which served as both arms and legs. The idea was for Mama to pull the limb of the monkey every day as a strengthening exercise to build up her muscle tone. When Mama grew tired, Sandy would help Mama pull the monkey's arm or leg. They loved to do that exercise together.

Both Sandy and I were inspired by Mama. Her life was truly a roller coaster of joy and sorrow, feat and defeat. Mama was blessed with beauty and intelligence, which helped her succeed in many ventures. However, she was cursed with poor health ever since she was young.

It started when she was living in Qingtian County, in southeastern China, and a parasite damaged her kidneys as a child. Mama had blood in her urine all the time, and the village doctor told her that it was unlikely she would ever have children. That diagnosis chased away many suitors. Eventually, though, Mama married an older businessman who did not care if she could not have children. Mama had no idea that her husband already had two sons and one daughter with another wife. Men were allowed to have multiple wives during those times in China.

Of course, the village doctor was a herbalist, not a medical doctor. He was wrong with his prediction that Mama would be barren. Mama was able to have four children after marrying my father when she was nineteen years old.

In 1965, three years after arriving in New York, Mama, Tina, and I were living in an apartment on 28th Street and 2nd Avenue, across the street from my Grandparents' apartment. Mama's persistent issues with bloody urine prompted her to seek medical help, so she went to Bellevue Hospital which was one block away. They realized the severity of Mama's condition, and immediately transferred her to Memorial Hospital on the Upper East Side of Manhattan. (Memorial Hospital merged with Sloan Kettering in 1980). The physicians there were very intrigued by Mama's condition. It was not a urinary tract infection or any other common urinary ailment. So, they performed a special procedure, inserting a tiny catheter in a vein on the top of each foot to enable a tiny camera to reach her kidneys, for a closer look.

They were amazed to find a parasite still living in her kidneys that they had never seen in America. Mama was brought to the lecture hall in front of the medical staff and students. She was so happy that so many people applauded her. Little did she realize that her fifteen minutes of fame was for having an unusual worm in her kidney. With medication to treat the parasitic infection, Mama was cured of her hematuria. Her health issues, though, were far from over.

Mama tried to work as a nurse for the dentist who sponsored our journey to America. However, she quickly had to seek other forms of employment because she did not speak English. Mama began working long hours in Chinese restaurants. She told us that the lunch menu was $0.95 from soup to desert. She would get a $0.05 tip per customer. She would earn a $0.25 tip from a dinner check. She saved all of her nickels and dimes. Six years after arriving in New York City, she was able to use her savings and put down a deposit for a townhouse in Flushing. She lived in that house from 1968 to 2022.

Whether it was the stress of working seventy hours a week or residual damage from her kidney disease, Mama developed high blood pressure and suffered several "mini strokes," or TIAs (Transient Ischemic Attacks). Eventually, she also developed four tumors, three of which were cancerous.

All of Mama's checkups, follow-ups, and tests were scheduled on different school holidays so I could accompany Mama and be there with her. I would take Phoebe and drive from Staten Island to Flushing, Queens. We picked up Mama and drove to Mt. Sinai Hospital in Manhattan to see her various specialists, which included a neurologist for her multiple TIAs, a cardiologist for her high blood pressure, and an endocrinologist for her hypothyroidism and osteoporosis.

The cardiologist was her primary doctor as well. He used to draw her blood himself and also performed the EKG, the electrocardiogram. The old leads were all colored coded. My Mama always laughed when the cardiologist placed the leads incorrectly. It turned out her cardiologist was colorblind.

After all the appointments were concluded, we would have a small lunch and drive back to Queens. Then, we would take Mama food shopping at the Chinese grocery store, have dinner in a restaurant, take Mama home, and drive back to Staten Island. A school holiday spent like this was more tiring than a workday and took more than the eight hours I normally worked as a teacher.

In 1998, Mama had her first surgery to remove a benign tumor from her stomach. She had two more surgeries, one to remove a cancerous tumor from her colon in 2004 and the other to remove a cancerous tumor from her breast in 2015. The fourth tumor was found in her stomach again but was left untreated because Mama was ninety-three years old and too weak to undergo any aggressive treatment.

Throughout all those years, I was always the designated driver, caretaker, and health proxy. While it was always challenging, the last six months of Mama's life were very difficult for me.

After being diagnosed with her second bout of stomach cancer, Mama was given hospice home care. To make her more comfortable, I trained the home aide how to cook, clean, and care for her.

One dish, in particular, that I insisted that the home aides make for Mama was dumplings, her favorite dish. Mama made the best dumplings with very thin skins and deliciously seasoned fillings. She learned to make them while she was working in the Chinese restaurants. She could make a hundred dumplings in an hour, each pleated exactly the same way. She also learned from the chefs how to make many other very delicious Chinese dishes.

Each of the seven successive home aides we hired for Mama made the dumplings differently. Mama would critique the dumplings for their appearance, flavor, and thickness of the wrapper. Each aide was overjoyed when they got a thumbs up and a smile from Mama. Unfortunately, that was not very often because no one could make dumplings like Mama.

Toward the end of her life, Mama developed a condition called nocturia. She would get up at least ten times a night to urinate, usually only a few drops each time. It was a condition that required someone to help her get up all those times throughout the night, and it obviously affected her sleep and quality of life. I realized then that it was not enough just to have everyone rotate sleeping over to care for her at night. We had to hire someone to care for Mama twenty-four hours seven days a week. Her health insurance only paid for seventy-eight hours per week of home care.

Due to her condition, Mama had lost a lot of weight and had no appetite. Her stomach tumor was bleeding and caused black stools every day. The internist noticed that her hemoglobin level from a blood test was very low and ordered a blood transfusion. (Hospice allowed only one blood transfusion, though.)

To receive the transfusion, Mama had to be transported to Northwell Health in Valley Stream in Long Island, New York. It was the longest and most miserable day for both of us. After this experience, we agreed—no more hospitals.

To start with, it took hours for the blood work and blood typing to be completed. Mama had very small veins, and a phlebotomist had to come with a sonogram and a heating pad to help locate a viable vein for the transfusion. Finally, after multiple attempts, an IV was correctly set up and only one bag of blood was hung on the IV stand for her transfusion.

The cardiac monitor kept beeping because her blood pressure and heart rate were tanking. Mama had had blood transfusions before, but this time was literally a life-and-death situation. Her arm was black and blue from all the failed IV attempts. Her weight had dropped to only seventy-two pounds; she was literally just skin and bones. Her ashen face and deep sunken eyes made us fear the worst for her.

The nonchalant resident said that this might be Mama's time to go. She was going to do nothing and let Mama die since Mama had signed a "Do Not Resuscitate" form.

"She is not dying today!" I yelled. "I am going to get my daughter to come here. You obviously don't know what you are doing," I said heatedly.

Phoebe is a pediatrician. When she arrived at the hospital, she took one look at the blood transfusion setup and immediately told the resident to give Mama a bag of saline. Mama hadn't eaten all day and no one had bothered to keep her fed or hydrated before the transfusion. She'd been at the hospital for twelve hours! Phoebe also demanded dinner and extra juice be sent to the room.

It was very painful and exhausting waiting for Mama's heart rate and blood pressure to normalize, but they eventually did. Phoebe went home after she saw Mama open her eyes and smile at her. Then Mama and I had to wait for the ambulance to come and transport us back home.

For some unknown reason, the two "experienced and well-trained" EMTs had locked their keys inside the ambulance while preparing Mama for transport. How could this happen? I wondered why Murphy's Law was always disrupting and ruining my days. I couldn't believe how so many unexpected things always seem to happen to me.

"Could you pick on someone else for a change?" I asked the heavens. "Why do you always make my day worse? When will you give me a break, Lord? I know I must have been a psychotic sociopath in my past life—but I swear I have repented. God, please forgive me and help me," I said, praying.

After her successful transfusion, Mama was clearly feeling better; she started yelling at me. She was furious, tired, and hated me for putting her through this ordeal. "Why don't you just put a pillow over my face? It would be more comfortable," Mama growled at me while clenching and gritting her teeth. "Tell them to drive me to a bridge, I want to jump off. It will be faster." Mama continued her bitter venting.

I listened quietly and shook my head slowly. "Not today. Mama. You are too tired to jump. I will drive you to a beautiful bridge another day. We can both jump off together." I was tired and frustrated with myself too.

I suddenly felt some fluid flowing down my face. *Is it raining? We are indoors. Is the ceiling leaking? No. What's this liquid on my face?* I was temporarily confused. *Oh no, is it tears? No way! What? How can I cry when I am so mad? How is it that I am crying at all?*

But then I realized what was happening. As the primary decision maker (and bearer of Mama's displeasure with my decisions), I had been through a lot. In that moment of fatigue and exhaustion, it was just the right time to cry. I realized I probably should have cried a long time ago.

I had been prescribed Xanax to control my anxiety years ago. Taking a Xanax and calling it a day had prevented me from crying for years. I could not cry even when I wanted to.

But that night, waiting with Mama for a second ambulance to rescue us, I dropped my shoulders and let out a deep sigh. Tears came rolling down, pouring out months of agony, anger, and aggravation.

"Thank you, God." I was relieved. I was finally able to release the heart-wrenching pain I had been carrying. The tears were able to wash away so much of my angst and anxiety. I began to sob.

When Mama saw how sad I was, she sighed loudly, and began to cry as well. I held her tiny black, blue and trembling hand and gave her a big hug. We both needed a good cry. Our tears were filled with sadness and pain. But we were also very happy that Mama was still alive at age ninety-three, despite having gone through three bouts of cancer.

We had to wait another hour for another ambulance to come. Altogether, it took fifteen hours that day for the travel, the waiting, the transfusion, and more waiting. That was indeed Mama's last hospital visit. Neither one of us could have survived another visit like that!

The blood transfusion worked. It gave Mama more energy for five more weeks. I soon scheduled separate lunch dates with all of Mama's relatives and friends so they could each come spend time with her. Both Mama and her guests all knew her days were limited. They were all very eager to spend these precious moments with each other. Everyone spoke kindly and praised Mama for all of her life's accomplishments. They admired how Mama took care of Grandpa after the passing of Grandma by paying for an old couple to live in our apartment on 28th street to cook and clean for Grandpa. They reminisce about the many good times they went through together. They remembered the friends and relatives who would be waiting for her in heaven. Many joked about Mama winning every mahjong game in the future and enjoying unlimited shark fin soup.

Mama was the happiest when her younger brother, Little Uncle Yao, visited with his family. Mama loved Little Uncle Yao and especially his son, Mitchell. Their multiple visits always cheered her up and brought her hope and joy. She wanted Mitchell to take anything he wanted in her house. Most of her porcelain or jade items were from Grandpa's gift shop. She wanted Mitchell to proudly carry on the family name and the tradition.

My Little Uncle Yao lived with our family in Shanghai from 1949 until 1957. He came to New York in 1959 at the age of nineteen with no skills or knowledge of the English language. He could not work in a restaurant because he did not speak English. He did not like working in the kitchen because the cooks spoke only Cantonese, and he spoke only Mandarin. He hated peddling slippers on street corners. To everyone's surprise, somehow, he managed to find a way to attend City College of New York, CCNY. He worked very hard to learn English and Electrical Engineering at the same time. He inherited the determination and intelligence from my grandfather. However, he did not like the business of importing or selling Chinese gifts and crafts that my grandfather had established.

It was really remarkable that Little Uncle Yao was able to apply and receive scholarships for his undergraduate and graduate studies. He was the first man from Qingtian, China to earn a PhD from CCNY. A PhD is the most prestigious degree and honor for a Chinese elite scholar. We called them Zhuangyuan (狀元). There was only one Zhuangyuan awarded each year in China from thousands of elite scholars who competed for this very esteemed honor. The Zhuangyuan was awarded with fame, fortune and political status.

The entire village in Qingtian and all of 28th Street in New York, were extremely proud of Little Uncle Yao. He was revered and respected by all those who knew him. My grandpa and my mom treated him with the highest esteem. When his son Mitchell was born, my grandpa expected another Zhuangyuan to further exalt the glory of the Jing family. Grandpa pampered and coddled Mitchell like a royal highness. He tried to teach Mitchell to memorize Chinese phrases from the *Three Character Classic* (三字經) when Mitchell was just three years old. Grandpa believed that these phrases epitomized the high morals one should understand and practice.

Mitchell hated the Chinese lessons. While he was reciting, he was literally pulling his hair out. He would twirl the few strands of hair on the top of his forehead and yank it out, resulting in a small round bald spot. He used his left hand to pick up food with the chopsticks. Grandpa would correct him right away by saying, "Normal people use their right hand to eat." Grandpa did not realize that he actually helped Mitchell become ambidextrous.

Both Little Uncle Yao and Mitchell worked for the famous think tank, Bell Labs, in New Jersey. They were both very successful. Little Uncle Yao became very wealthy from his multiple patents on fiber optics.

Mitchell changed his career from engineering to financial management and made even more money than his father. He owned multiple mansions, several expensive cars like Maserati and Bentley. He even owned *a few dozen* invisible, intangible but incredibly valuable Bitcoins.

As Mama was hosting her friends and family in her waning days, Mama's grandchildren brought a digital photo frame and installed a huge collection of precious moments with her friends and relatives from past to present. She enjoyed watching the continuously changing photos of everyone she knew. When she had energy and mental clarity, she would tell us a story here and there about this person or that situation. She remembered her visits to Paris, Germany, Belgium, and Taiwan. We were delighted to hear her stories about many relatives in faraway places.

The most memorable trip she took was with all of us in 2005 when we all visited China. My father's house in Shanghai had seven families living in it. The porcelain bathtub was where everyone washed their clothes. The clothes were hung and dried in the courtyard. The kindergarten was no longer there. One lady who still lived down the lane, remembered that my Mama was the "Needle Nurse". Mama used to bring home vaccines from the hospital and gave shots to the kids living nearby. Mama managed to score inexpensive hair and spa treatments and wonderful bargains with her cunning negotiation and haggling skills. She loved wearing the Burberry jacket she bought for $6.00.

Mama was energized and joyful after each visit from her brother and other relatives. She had plenty of energy to see all of her children, grandchildren, and her three great-grandchildren on Mother's Day on 5/8/2022. Everyone in her family came to see her and enjoyed a very bountiful and delicious lunch. Mama always wanted plenty of good food to treat her guests.

The best gift Mama received on her last Mother's day was from Grace, her grand-daughter-in law. Mama learned that her fourth great-grandchild was on his way.

"What child?" Sandy was confused.

"Your great grandma was ecstatic when your mother told her that you were going to have a little brother," I said to Sandy. Her brother, Timothy, was born in December that year.

It was a very good day indeed. She was surrounded by loved ones and many bouquets of orchids, roses, and carnations—all of her favorite flowers.

Eight days after Mother's Day in 2022, during her peaceful slumber, she left us and passed on to join the angels in heaven above. I am confident that she told all her friends, relatives, and angels, joyously and triumphantly,

"I have fought the good fight, I have finished the race, I have kept the faith." 2 Timothy 4:7 (NIV).

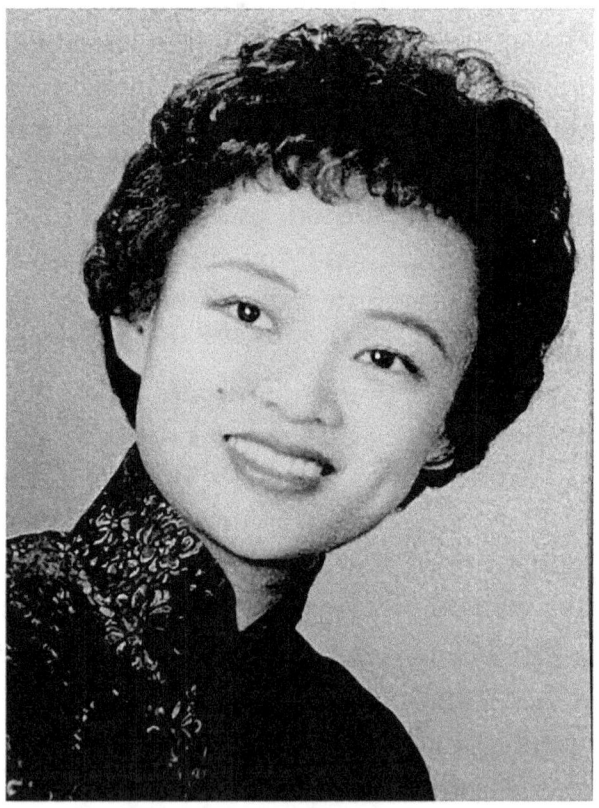

Photo of Mom

CHAPTER 15

MONKEY BUSINESS

Sandy loved to play with her stuffed monkeys. The monkey she liked the most was a green one whose arm was so long that it wrapped around her neck. She wore that monkey like a backpack. The tummy of the monkey had a pouch for her to keep her favorite stuffed animal, a once pink but now gray velour bunny.

I looked and laughed at her silliness and decided to tell her Chinese stories about monkeys, like the magical and powerful Monkey King and the famous Three Wise Monkeys. Sandy was born in the Year of the Monkey.

"Come sit with me, you cheeky monkey!" I said to her, enthusiastically.

"Cheeky monkey?" she asked, laughing.

"That's what the British call their lovely children."

"What do Chinese call their children?" asked Sandy.

"We call them, *Bao Bao* (寶寶), which means Jewel or *Xia Pun Yo*, (小朋友), which means Little Friend."

"Why would anyone call their children monkeys?"

"Because monkeys are smart, playful, and very mischievous."

"What's mischievous?" Sandy wondered.

"It means the person is making trouble and not following rules," I said.

"I am not mischievous. I follow rules."

"Yes, darling. You are an angel, even if you are mischievous some of the time."

"Is there a story about monkeys?" Sandy was curious.

"Of course. There are two stories about monkeys. The Monkey King and the Three Wise Monkeys. Which story would you like to hear first?"

"The Monkey King! Tell me all about it, Nai Nai." She was very happy.

"The Monkey King is the most cunning, powerful, and magical monkey," I said.

In the Chinese heavens, there was a magical peach tree. It produced delicious and powerful peaches every 3,000 years. The elixir of these giant and delicious peaches would provide vitality and immortality. Only the Chinese gods were allowed to eat them.

There were many magical and powerful animals living in the heavens, like dragons, phoenixes, and monkeys. One of the monkeys was very curious, very bright, and always scheming. One day, it stole one of the special peaches and enjoyed it very much. It then continued to eat more peaches until it ate half of the peaches on the tree.

The Eight Immortal Gods and the Heavenly Emperor were very angry and wanted to capture and kill the monkey—but the peaches gave the monkey immortality! The monkey wreaked havoc all over heaven when the celestial guards were chasing it. The Heavenly Emperor decided to punish the monkey by sending it to live on Earth. It was assigned to protect an extremely devout and pure-at-heart Buddhist monk who was traveling to India to receive a holy scroll about Buddhism.

While the monkey had magical powers and immortality, it was also very mischievous. The Heavenly Emperor cast a very strong spell on it to control it when it misbehaved. The Heavenly Emperor told the monk what to chant when the monkey disobeyed.

"What did the chant do to the monkey?" asked Sandy.

"The chant gave the monkey a super-duper, extremely excruciating, painful headache. We call it a migraine now."

"Wow, that hurts. Mommy has to lie down when she gets one of those migraine headaches," said Sandy.

"That was the only way to control the monkey. Meanwhile, the monkey protected the monk from all sorts of evil spirits and helped the monk to bring the holy scroll for Buddhism safely to China."

"Why is he called the Monkey King?"

"Because this monkey was the most powerful and enchanted of all the monkeys in the world. It could defeat many enemies and perform many magic tricks, like disappearing into thin air."

"Wow. That's a great monkey." Sandy hugged her green monkey and said, "You are my monkey king."

"Do you want to hear about the other monkey story?" I asked.

"Yes, Nai Nai. Are they all magical, too?"

"Not magical, but they are smart."

"How smart?"

"Well, you tell me if you think they are smart," I told her.

"Okay."

"There were three monkeys sitting on a log. One used its two hands and covered its eyes. The second one covered its ears. And the third one covered its mouth," I said.

"Why did they do that?" she asked.

"The one who covered its eyes said that it does not see evil."

"Is it blind or can it see something else?" Sandy was curious.

"You can tell me what you think when I finish the story," I said. "The second monkey with its ears covered said that it hears no evil."

"What did the third monkey say?" Sandy asked.

"Well, the third monkey had its mouth covered, so it could not speak. The other two monkeys spoke for it. They said that the third monkey does not speak evil."

"So, one monkey was blind, the second was deaf, and the third monkey was mute. What's so special about that? They are not smart!" Sandy said, laughing.

"According to Confucius, the very wise Chinese philosopher who started all the good Chinese traditions, the three monkeys represent three wise things not to do," I said.

"What things?"

"The monkey who covered its eyes suggests that we should not see any improper things that might tempt us to do something bad," I said.

"What improper things?"

"Sometimes, when we see other people's riches, it might create jealousy, greed, or hatred in us."

"Is jealousy bad?" Sandy said.

"Only if it makes you want to do something bad to the person that you are jealous of," I said.

"What does the deaf monkey want us to do?"

"That monkey does not want us to hear gossip or lies."

"That's smart," said Sandy.

"The mute monkey is one who does not speak poorly of anyone. He does not tell lies or say bad things about others."

"I guess he is smart too."

"The three monkeys represent three good behaviors. That's why they are called the Three Wise Monkeys."

"Oh, I see," said Sandy.

"Yes, my love. To be a wise person, we must not see greed or hatred. We must not listen to lies or false pretenses. And we must not say bad things or curse words," I told her.

"I can do that. Will that make me a wise person?"

"Absolutely. You know, there is a new interpretation of the Three Wise Monkeys." I added.

"What do you mean?"

"Like all things, different people can see and hear things differently. The modern version of the Three Wise Monkeys is that they do the right things instead of not doing the wrong things."

"Huh? I don't understand." Sandy looked very puzzled.

"There was a man named Gandhi. He was an Indian leader who wanted India to be free from British rule. He thought the monkeys should represent what to do instead of what not to do."

"He thought the three wise monkeys should see the truth, hear the truth, and speak the truth, especially about how the Indian people were being treated," I said.

"That's so much easier to understand. I like that!" Sandy said excitedly.

"Good. My darling Sandy, you will grow up to be a very kind and wise person. I am so proud of you."

"Will these monkeys still have to cover their mouths and ears?" Sandy was puzzled.

"No, I guess. The new version of wise monkeys would not cover their eyes, mouths and ears. They have to see, hear and speak the truth." I replied after pondering.

Sandy went to play with her monkey, and I sighed as I reflected on the number of people who were born in the year of the monkey in my own life. I was born in the year of the tiger. According to the Chinese Zodiac, people born in the year of the tiger were incompatible with people who were born in the year of the monkey.

There was some truth to that. Of course, there were also exceptions. My grandmother and my granddaughter were born in the year of the monkey. We are very close and definitely compatible.

However, there were also many people born in the year of the monkey who were totally incomprehensible to me and had values or behavior in complete opposition to mine.

Interestingly, one such person is my husband, William. I think the western culture of Opposite Attracts must be the reason why we married. We were drawn together when we were young and foolishly blinded by love.

But the Chinese Zodiac was completely correct beyond any doubts. He and I literally were day and night in terms of our philosophies and lifestyles. I had no idea that he was a pessimist and a procrastinator. He liked to lounge back and analyze problems and worried about the negative consequences. I wanted to march forward to solve problems immediately with hope of a positive outcome.

Throughout our fifty years of marriage, we had the propensity to disagree and debate all matters, trivial and significant. We always dismissed each other's opinions or wishes. If I said let's do this today, he said let's do it tomorrow.

If I said to discard something, he saved it as a souvenir. If I said turn left, he turned right. Even though we have a modern GPS system in our car, we still have to make many K-turns and U-turns. That's why we are always late to all events.

To stay harmonious in my marriage meant that I would need to say and do the exact opposite of my own wishes, so that William, who would always do the opposite to what I said, would ultimately do just the thing I originally wanted him to do. That was very exhausting and too much strategizing for my muddled and fuddled brain.

After fifty years of heated arguments, aggressive discussion, and hostile debates, we have both learned to cohabitate by following the wisdom of the Three Wise Monkeys.

When we each want to do things our own way or speak our own mind, it aggravates the other person. We have accepted that we are not compatible. Therefore, like the wise monkeys, we don't see or hear the "improper" actions and words of the other person. We only see and hear our own "truth." As for the lousy words that we used to scream loudly at one another, we no longer speak evil to each other. We only speak the truth, our truth, or we don't speak to each other at all.

After all, he is always right, but I am never wrong. We get along just fine now, especially since we have complete control of the volume on our own hearing aids.

What Is Your Chinese Zodiac Sign?
(Chinese Zodiac Chart)

Rat	Ox	Tiger	Rabbit	Dragon	Snake	Horse	Sheep	Monkey	Rooster	Dog	Pig
1912	1913	1914	1915	1916	1917	1918	1919	1920	1921	1922	1923
1924	1925	1926	1927	1928	1929	1930	1931	1932	1933	1934	1935
1936	1937	1938	1939	1940	1941	1942	1943	1944	1945	1946	1947
1948	1949	1950	1951	1952	1953	1954	1955	1956	1957	1958	1959
1960	1961	1962	1963	1964	1965	1966	1967	1968	1969	1970	1971
1972	1973	1974	1975	1976	1977	1978	1979	1980	1981	1982	1983
1984	1985	1986	1987	1988	1989	1990	1991	1992	1993	1994	1995
1996	1997	1998	1999	2000	2001	2002	2003	2004	2005	2006	2007
2008	2009	2010	2011	2012	2013	2014	2015	2016	2017	2018	2019
2020	2021	2022	2023	2024	2025	2026	2027	2028	2029	2030	2031
2032	2033	2034	2035	2036	2037	2038	2039	2040	2041	2042	2043

https://www.travelchinaguide.com/intro/chinese-zodiac-years-chart.
htm?srsltid=AfmBOorSvznxGO11cV47D0TgrlpgjEadaJlEMYAf2Gvl4Lkq55Et8unq

Chinese Zodiac Compatibility Chart

Animal Sign	Best Match	Just So-so	Worst Match
Rat	Ox, Dragon, Monkey	Rat, Tiger	Horse, Rooster
Ox	Rat, Snake, Rooster	Ox, Monkey	Tiger, Dragon, Horse, Sheep
Tiger	Dragon, Horse, Pig	Rat, Rabbit	Ox, Tiger, Snake, Monkey
Rabbit	Sheep, Monkey, Dog, Pig	Tiger, Rabbit, Dragon, Horse	Snake, Rooster
Dragon	Rooster, Rat, Monkey	Rabbit, Horse	Ox, Sheep, Dog
Snake	Dragon, Rooster	Dog	Tiger, Rabbit, Snake, Sheep, Pig
Horse	Tiger, Sheep, Rabbit	Rabbit, Dragon, Monkey, Dog	Rat, Ox, Rooster, Horse
Sheep	Horse, Rabbit, Pig	Rooster	Ox, Tiger, Dog
Monkey	Ox, Rabbit	Horse, Rooster	Tiger, Pig
Rooster	Ox, Snake	Sheep, Monkey, Pig	Rat, Rabbit, Horse, Rooster, Dog
Dog	Rabbit	Ox, Snake, Horse, Dog	Dragon, Sheep, Rooster
Pig	Tiger, Rabbit, Sheep	Rooster	Snake, Monkey

https://www.travelchinaguide.com/intro/social_customs/zodiac/compatibility.
htm?srsltid=AfmBOorJwkd8ncaVb8ciOtrRMDuYC1UfvgrzIPtbNkWDEgQiHrAkiDLq

CHAPTER 16

THE MISUNDERSTOOD

Sandy was eight years old when I took her to Lincoln Center in Manhattan in 2024 to see a special performance of Chinese dances by the Shen Yun dance troupe. I wanted her to see the dance about the Monkey King. It was a very exciting and novel experience for her and a great chance to see and experience things she had never seen before, like the synchronized water fountain show in Lincoln Center and the hustling and bustling of the city life.

We took the Long Island Railroad to Penn Station. The ride was comfortable, quiet, and smooth. Passengers were relaxed and dressed appropriately for work. Some men wore ties. Most of the women wore high heels. We were able to sit throughout the ride. Each stop was announced.

Walking through Penn Station was an eye-opener for Sandy. She saw musicians playing their instruments, like a guitar or a violin, and people tossing money into their open instrument cases.

"Why do they play here?" asked Sandy.

"Not everyone can play in theaters."

"Do they make money this way?"

"I think so. They have to compete with other musicians to get a permit to play here."

Sandy looked thoughtful. "Is this a good job?"

"It is, if you like to play your favorite kind of music every day with no one complaining or judging you, no one to look over your shoulder, and no one to boss you around."

"Don't they get hot and tired?"

"That is the best part of the job. They can pack up and go home whenever they want."

We listened to a guitarist playing and singing one of Taylor Swift's songs, *Shake it off.* I gave Sandy a dollar to put into the guitar case. We then walked briskly to the A train.

Getting onto the A train was an adventure. I told Sandy never to stand close to the tracks to avoid being pushed into the path of an oncoming train by deranged people. She held my hand tightly and asked questions quietly as she looked at the variety of people congregating on the platform.

"Why are so many people wearing hats and scarves when it is so hot down here?"

"Hats represent so many things. You know, some hats tell you what kind of job a person has. The police, the firemen, and construction workers all wear hats."

"But these are not those hats, these hats have different shapes and are made of cloth."

"Those head coverings usually represent someone's religion or tradition. A yarmulke is worn by a man who is Jewish. Turbans or scarves can be worn by many types of people like Indians, Africans, and Arabs for their tradition."

"Wow, I had no idea so many people have special things to wear." Sandy was surprised to learn of the different apparel for different religions and cultures. "It's like great-grandma wearing the Chinese dress during Chinese New Year," she added.

As the A train approached the station, Sandy and I noticed that the subway train was much dirtier and squeakier than the Long Island Railroad train. When we boarded the train, we noticed it was very crowded and that there were no seats available. Sandy wrapped her arms around my waist as I held onto the strap hanger. The train made many quick stops without any announcements. People were rushing in and out of the doors. They all looked very stressed and hurried.

Sandy had a worried look on her tiny pretty face. She didn't expect so many people to be coming and going so quickly. No one was smiling. Most people had blank looks on their face. Many looked really busy, tapping on their cell phones constantly. She finally asked quietly the quintessential question, "Are we there yet?"

We finally reached our stop. As we climbed the stairs out of the station and back into the sunlight, she was shocked to see the streets were so crowded with people, bikes, motorbikes, trucks, and cars. Pedestrians were moving in haste. The sounds of sirens were blaring.

"Oh my gosh, it is so loud!" Sandy was shell shocked.

"Yes, I know. You have never seen this many cars and people in your quiet neighborhood."

"Is it always this way?"

"Oh yes, and during the holiday seasons, it's even worse. That's why the city sets aside a few streets where only people can walk and shop, and no cars are allowed."

"There are so many cars here. But why are the cars not moving?" Sandy asked curiously.

"Do you see all the street signs?"

"Oh yeah. There are so many signs everywhere."

"The drivers must look at all the signs. That's one of the reasons why they have to drive slower. Another reason is that so many people are crossing the streets, some at the corner, some in the middle of the road. Cars have to move very carefully not to hit anyone."

"Why is there a bicycle drawing on the street?'

"Oh well, that's another reason to slow down. The ground that was painted with a bicycle means only bicycle riders can use it." I pointed to the bike lane and continued to explain the bus lane, the turn lane, and of course, the most precious of all lanes, the parking lane.

"Oh my gosh. Which lane is for driving?"

"Usually, the middle two lanes are available for cars and trucks. And if one truck is parked for delivery, then there is only one lane for driving."

"I think it's faster to walk," she sighed.

People wearing unusual clothing really intrigued Sandy. Many men were topless. Some wore gym outfits. Some wore business suits. Some women wore very revealing "mini-shorts and mini-skirts." Yet, some seemed to be all wrapped in cloth.

"Why are these ladies all wrapped up in black?" She noticed some women wearing burqas.

"They might be from the Middle East because the burqa is the dress for women of the Muslim religion."

"They must be burning up, all wrapped up like that." She scratched her head.

"Actually, no. The black cloth is made of a gauzy material or chiffon. It is light and airy."

"Oh, Nai, Nai, look. Look at that woman all wrapped in gold." She pointed at an Indian woman wearing a sari.

"It's not nice to point. That is one long piece of light silk arranged into a dress called a sari that is worn by women of India and other countries in that part of the world."

"I think I am Catholic. What type of things should I wear?" Sandy asked.

"Some Catholics wear veils when they go to church, but not outside the church."

"What religion are you, Nai Nai?"

"I am a Christian. I don't wear or do anything special for my religion."

"What does that mean?"

"That means I believe in the Almighty God and that I have to do good and be good. I don't have to wear anything fancy or complicated."

"Wow. That sounds really easy to follow."

"Yes, and you are a wonderfully kind person because you believe in God."

Sandy was also impressed by the many different kinds of food carts selling hot dogs, kabobs, nuts, ice cream and pretzels. Of course, she had to taste the soft, salty, and oversized pretzel.

"Where is the M&M's store? Nai Nai, you promised that I can buy fifty different colored candies."

"Yes, after the show, I promise. You can buy two of each color of the M&M's candies. But there are only fifteen different colors, not fifty. When we go to Times Square, you will also see some people wearing really crazy outfits."

"What crazy outfits?" She was overjoyed at the thought of seeing even more interesting outfits.

"Street performers dress up like robots, the Statue of Liberty, Mickey Mouse, and even Superheroes."

"What do they perform?"

"Some sing, some dance, and some just walk about or stand around, waiting for people to take photos with them and give them money."

"Oh Nai Nai, look. That lady is being dragged," she shouted as she pointed to a dog walker holding a bouquet of different colored leashes belonging to a pack of several dogs running ahead of her.

"Oh, don't worry. She is not being dragged. She is walking the dogs." I explained.

"That's a lot of dogs to walk. Look, there are five dogs. Three of them are huge."

"Oh, yes. That is another job for some people in New York City."

"Is that a good job?"

"Well, I would not recommend it."

"Why?"

"The person has to walk or run after lots of dogs. As each dog poops, the person has to pick up the poop and throw it away."

"Yuck! I do not like that job!"

As we walked a few more blocks, we saw a dirty and unkempt person sitting on the street holding a broken cup, asking for money. Another squalid person with lots of plastic bags around him was sleeping on a nearby corner.

"Why are they sitting and sleeping on the dirty street?" Sandy questioned.

"These people have no money and no place to sleep," I sighed.

"That is so sad."

I gave Sandy one dollar to put inside the cup held up by the homeless man.

"Thank you. Bless you." He was grateful and smiled, showing his blackened teeth.

Sandy was frightened and speedily returned to my side and held my hand tightly. As we quickly walked away, I said gently to Sandy, "You just did a good deed."

"Really?"

"Yes. You were kind to him."

"But it's your money."

"It doesn't matter. You saw how your kindness made him smile."

"He smelled awful."

"Sorry, my honey-bunny. He has no place to shower. I want you to know that we must be kind to the unfortunate people."

"Why are they like this?"

"No one knows exactly what happened to them. Some of them became poor or homeless because they are addicted to drugs or alcohol. Some of them are mentally unwell. Some of them lost their jobs or lost their families."

"I don't understand." Sandy lowered her head and shook it a little.

"It's okay. There are lots of things I don't understand, either."

"What? You don't understand some things?" She was surprised.

"Sure. I don't understand why some people have no luck, like some of the homeless people. Why do some veterans become homeless? Why are some young people plagued by cancer and dying young? Why are some people blessed and others cursed? Why did the innocent people perish and the evil ones live long and prosper?" I was venting my own frustration. "But, you don't have to understand all the troubles in the world now. It is important that you know not everyone is lucky to have good health, good jobs, a good house, or a place to shower or sleep."

"I feel bad for these people." Sandy was concerned.

"It is very good that you are concerned for these less fortunate people. When you grow up a little more, you will learn more about how to help them."

I was very happy that she saw many different types of people that day. I hoped she learned that it was okay not to understand how some people dressed or what job they had, and to be curious to learn more. Many people are misunderstood because we do not know their background or their life experience. It would be great if she learned that we must always do our best to be kind. It doesn't matter where others come from or what religion they believe in.

Meanwhile, in my heart, I was thinking of the most misunderstood person in our family—me. Many of my relatives have thought of me as senile and silly. Some people have even thought that I am certifiably insane.

"You know something I really don't understand, my darling Sandy?"

"What?" She looked at me with wonderment.

"I don't understand why everyone thinks I am crazy."

"Well, Nai Nai, sometimes you say strange things," she explained. "You can never get the right name for the person you are talking to."

"Well, that's because there are too many names to remember," I explained.

The names of all the children in the family are cycled through my tiny brain before I land on the right name for the child standing in front of me. The children used to be very annoyed, believing I did not care for them. After a while, though, they understood how my brain was thinking faster than my mouth could speak. They knew to expect at least three or four wrong names before their correct name was announced. They now think of me as eccentric, not crazy. If I speak their name on the first try, they give me a round of applause and a thumbs up.

More often than not, when I speak, names and places are left out or misspoken. I once said, after wanting to move on from disappointment, "Forget it, the bridge is under the water." What I meant to say was, "Forget it, it's water under the bridge."

Some of my misspoken phrases puzzle the listeners, but they usually quickly realize my mistakes. I once said, "Happy Yarmulke." It was easy to understand that I meant, "Happy Hanukkah." With all these linguistic mix-ups, I guess it's no wonder everyone in my family thought I was senile and suffered from dementia.

My students, in addition to learning science, also had to learn to adapt to my verbal gymnastics. I once told them about the survival of the fittest. "He who survives would perish." Of course, they were shocked to hear that. But it did not take long for them to know that I meant, "He who survives would flourish."

Another aspect about me that is often misunderstood is my pure intention to help people. I've always wanted to do the right thing and help others. Unfortunately, many people think of my help as a form of control or meddling. The way I try to solve problems seems redundant to many people and sometimes, my solution only exacerbates the problem. It has been said that the road to hell is paved with good intentions. It seems very possible that I will be going to hell in my afterlife.

In April 2018, my daughter Phoebe wanted to volunteer with an organization to bring medical care to orphans in Nanjing, China. I wanted to help protect her. I bought pepper spray and a stun gun for her to take with her for self-defense. She thought these gifts were unnecessary, since she was traveling with a group of physicians and the philanthropic organization was endorsed by the Chinese government. However, being the ever vigilant mother, I insisted she take these items with her for added protection.

Her flight was not a direct flight. She stopped over in Hong Kong for a six-hour layover. She had to go through customs. Little did we know that these self-defense items were deemed illegal in Hong Kong.

Eight police officers escorted my frightened and furious daughter to the police precinct near the airport, transporting her in a huge police van with its sirens blaring and lights flashing. An arrest record was registered, as were her fingerprints. She was jailed in a dirty, small cell with no toilets or sinks. They respected her enough to give her a tiny filthy jail cell all to herself.

The philanthropic organization that sponsored the group of American surgeons and physicians to Nanjing could not help my daughter at all. I could not understand why. Instead, they called me in NY to let me know that Phoebe was being detained by the Hong Kong police. What?!

"Who should I call? What should I do? Who do I know in Hong Kong?" I panicked. The organizer said they would talk to the police but promised nothing. They must continue on to Nanjing.

One of the sergeants at the police precinct spoke very good English and explained the whole situation to Phoebe and told her how best to proceed. Her status of being a pediatrician volunteering to help Chinese children from an orphanage impressed the sergeants. They released her after she paid a bail of $2000 HKD, approximately $258 USD. She had to come back and appear in a Hong Kong court to plead her case in front of a judge. The court date was yet to be determined.

Thank God Phoebe had added the international call feature to her cell phone service. She called from Hong Kong to curse in my ears, chastising me in no uncertain terms on how my stun gun stunned her. She was flabbergasted and abhorred at how she was treated. The legal fees and the flight back to appear in court would be at my expense.

Phoebe's trip to Nanjing with a team of surgeons was to help evaluate children with correctable orthopedic conditions. The most severe surgery was for a fourteen-year old boy with severe spinal scoliosis. The team prepared him for the ten-hour surgery to straighten his spine. The before and after X-rays showed incredible progress. The young man literally gained six inches in height in one day. The success of this surgery and dozens of other repairs for cleft palates were very rewarding for her, even though she did not perform the surgeries.

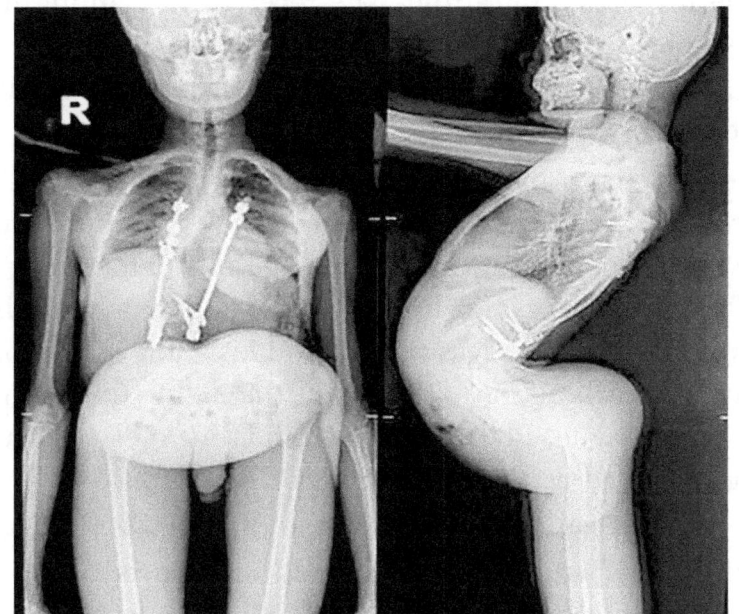

Before surgery

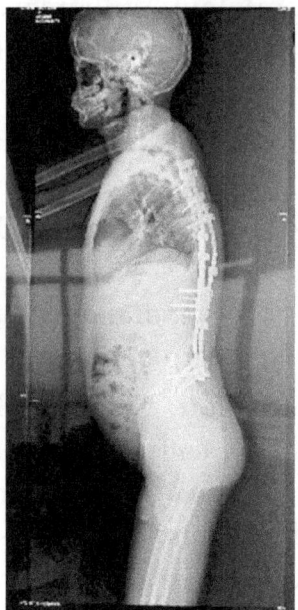

After surgery

X-Ray of Before and After Surgery of Spine Sclerosis

The respect and gratitude she received in Nanjing helped to ease her big trouble in little Hong Kong. But when she came home, she demanded that I fix and expunge her criminal record.

I called the American Embassy in Hong Kong, a local congressman, and many attorney friends who gave me the name of an American attorney in Hong Kong. It took four years and $4000 USD to resolve this misunderstanding. In hindsight, it would have cost far less money and less time if Phoebe had the street smarts to pay off each of the eight cops with $100 USD. To this date, Phoebe still reminds me, very frequently, how I destroyed her life with my good intentions.

Another person I almost killed with my care and concern is my dear husband William. He has always loved a dish made with sauerkraut and pork belly that his mom used to make. I thought I could improve that dish by replacing the fatty pork belly with very lean pork loin. William was thrilled that I tried to cook his favorite dish. He happily gobbled down the dish for two nights and developed a small bout of the hiccups.

We paid no attention to the hiccups until two full weeks had passed and he was still hiccupping. He was very uncomfortable and was also having difficulty breathing. Having exhausted all methods to relieve the hiccups, such as drinking water, sudden surprises, holding his breath, and even standing on his head, we decided to go to the emergency room.

The physician said there was a build up of acid in his stomach, which somehow caused a diaphragm strain. He was given a shot of steroids and was prescribed antacids and a muscle relaxant. The hiccups finally dissipated after another week. Poor William told me and thanked me in advance never to cook that dish again. Apparently, the fatty pork belly was necessary to absorb the acid from the sauerkraut. Who knew!

My son Justin was also not spared from the maligned outcomes of my good intentions. He had a notebook that I gave him. I had no idea there was a $100 bill tucked in the pocket of the back cover. Justin found the bill and asked me if I put it there. I said no and told him that it was his lucky day that he found the money. He decided to keep it for luck.

A few months later, he joined his friends at the Mohegan Sun casino in Connecticut. He decided to use his lucky $100 on the roulette wheel. He was so happy that he won $36.00 when one of the many numbers that he bet on came through, not realizing that he just lost $64.00.

His happiness was quickly squashed and excitement crushed. Two security guards approached him and escorted him to the office in the back of the casino. His friends were dumbfounded and did not know what to do, "Should we get a lawyer?"

"No. Don't worry. I didn't do anything wrong." Justin told his friends as he was led away.

After thirty minutes of intense interrogation, Justin was allowed back into the casino. His friends surrounded him cheerfully and asked for an immediate and detailed update. Justin took the free alcoholic drinks held by two of his friends and swallowed them down in two big gulps.

"I don't know how they know. But it's amazing," Justin explained.

"What's amazing?" One friend asked.

"The bill I gave the dealer when I was playing roulette was a counterfeit."

"Oh, no!" his friends gasped.

"Oh, yes. It was a counterfeit bill. They showed me how the colors were off."

"Oh, no. Are they arresting you?"

"They would have, had I not lied to save myself."

"What lie?"

"I told them that I got the bill from a local merchant."

"Where *did* you get that *shit*?" another friend asked.

"I found it in a notebook that my mom gave me."

"Oh, no!" they all sighed.

"Oh, yes. I will have a very long talk with her about this. You bet."

To this date, I have no idea who put that bill in that notebook. Phoebe was delighted to learn of Justin's misadventure. She was not alone in getting into trouble with the law on account of me.

It seems that my heart and brain always want to help others. However, my jumbled words and humble actions don't always reflect any wisdom or assistance. They usually muddle the message and create more chaos. That's why everyone thinks of me as crazy.

I think many of my life experiences have permanently damaged my brain. The forgetting of names definitely resulted from having thousands of student names to remember during twenty-five years of teaching. The very small storage area in the prefrontal cortex of my brain really could not retain any information for long. All those names and stories and other information were all co-mingling together, resulting in mismatched or incoherent thought processes. I think that's why I often misspeak or combine two or more thoughts together, uttering mumble jumble rubbish that no one can understand.

Perhaps I should learn that not everyone needs or seeks my help. On some occasions, the right thing to do is to do nothing at all and let nature take its course. Everyone needs to find their own path and experience their own failures and victories.

No one would want or like a nagging and nosy granny telling them what to do all of the time, I remind myself.

On our way home, I tried to remind Sandy how to interpret what we encountered that day. The most important thing that I hoped Sandy learned was the need to be good no matter how different others looked. "You know, my darling Sandy, if you remove all the clothing and hats, you will see that everyone is really the same. Just imagine that you are in a big pool with lots of children."

"Yeah, everyone looks the same, all soaking wet," Sandy confirmed with a smile.

"You know, a very wise woman, Maya Angelou said, "We can learn to see each other and see ourselves in each other and recognize that human beings are more alike than we are unalike.""

"She is right," agreed Sandy.

I calmly reassured her. "We don't always know where some people come from, or why they do what they do, or why they look different. But they are still people, just like you and me."

"Yes, Nai Nai. I know everyone is different. I will be good. I won't make fun of them for being different."

"Don't forget to be like the wise monkey and always do the right thing," I added.

"Yes, Nai Nai. I will do the right thing. One right thing to do is always wear matching shoes." Sandy laughed wholeheartedly, reminding me of my mistakes. It was a very good day.

"Nai, Nai, please tell me another story about yourself. All of your stories are so interesting," Sandy asked while we were going home, sitting on cushioned seats riding on the clean Long Island Railroad train.

"There are many more stories to tell and many historic events to learn about. The most important thing that I hope you understand from what we experienced is that we have to be good and do good."

"Yes, Nai Nai."

"I also hope that you will remember some of the Chinese traditions, Chinese holidays, and of course, Chinese foods that we have."

"Yes, Nai Nai. I love Chinese New Year. I get lots of red envelopes. Egg rolls, and Peking duck are my favorite foods."

"You know, instead of me telling you another story, how about I read you a poem that I wrote just for you and your brother. It's about being kind."

"Oh yes. That's great. Can I read it to Timothy?"

"Sure. If you like it, I will make it into a children's book."

"I know I'll like it. I love the book that you wrote about me and my Bunny Boo. I can't wait to read another book *all about me* to my friends."

Let Your Heart Be Your Guide

Life is not always fair or kind,
Its true meaning is hard to find.
Some burdens feel too much to bear—
Still, do your best with tender care.

Not every wish will come to light,
Some dreams may vanish out of sight.
But don't let sorrow pull you low—
Let your heart guide where you go.

Not every day brings light and cheer,
And not all storms are cause for fear.
Embrace the best, endure the worst,
Live with purpose—be well-versed.

Some may look different on the outside,
But we're all the same on the inside.
No need to judge, or scorn, or hate—
Treat cach soul as a friend or mate.

Let your heart guide your way.
Kindness brightens every day.
Being kind is brave and true—
Love and peace will follow you.

"Kindness is a language which the deaf can hear, and the blind can see." —Mark Twain

REFERENCES

Pletcher, K. (2025, February 13). Opium Wars. Encyclopedia Britannica. https://www.britannica.com/topic/Opium-Wars

Wu, Yuning. "Chinese Exclusion Act". Encyclopedia Britannica, 11 Jan. 2025, https://www.britannica.com/topic/Chinese-Exclusion-Act

The Editors of Encyclopedia Britannica (2025, April 26). First Sino-Japanese War. Encyclopedia Britannica. https://www.britannica.com/event/First-Sino-Japanese-War-1894-1895

The Editors of Encyclopedia Britannica (2003, March 19). Boxer Rebellion summary. Encyclopedia Britannica. https://www.britannica.com/summary/Boxer-Rebellion

The Editors of Encyclopedia Britannica (2025, February 13). Boxer Rebellion. Encyclopedia Britannica. https://www.britannica.com/event/Boxer-Rebellion

https://earlychinesemit.mit.edu/three-waves/boxer-indemnity-scholarship-program/

https://backstagehistory.substack.com/p/welcome-to-backstage?utm_campaign=post&utm_medium=web

https://backstagehistory.substack.com/p/from-rebellion-to-reform-the-boxer?r=4l7p3z&triedRedirect=true

https://backstagehistory.substack.com/p/tsinghua-university-born-from-diplomacy?utm_campaign=post&utm_medium=web

The Editors of Encyclopedia Britannica (2024, March 22). May Fourth Movement. Encyclopedia Britannica. https://www.britannica.com/event/May-Fourth-Movement

The Editors of Encyclopedia Britannica (2018, February 1). Shandong question. Encyclopedia Britannica. https://www.britannica.com/event/Shandong-question

Wang, Y.C. (2025, May 13). Sun Yat-sen. Encyclopedia Britannica. https://www.britannica.com/biography/Sun-Yat-sen

Schram, S.R. (2025, May 3). Mao Zedong. Encyclopedia Britannica. https://www.britannica.com/biography/Mao-Zedong

The Editors of Encyclopedia Britannica (2025, May 7). Chiang Kai-shek. Encyclopedia Britannica. https://www.britannica.com/biography/Chiang-Kai-shek

The Editors of Encyclopedia Britannica (2025, May 10). Manchukuo. Encyclopedia Britannica. https://www.britannica.com/place/Manchukuo

The Editors of Encyclopedia Britannica (2025, March 27). Second Sino-Japanese War. Encyclopedia Britannica. https://www.britannica.com/event/Second-Sino-Japanese-War

The Editors of Encyclopedia Britannica (2024, November 25). Marco Polo Bridge Incident. Encyclopedia Britannica. https://www.britannica.com/event/Marco-Polo-Bridge-Incident

Swift, J. (2024, December 11). Mukden Incident. Encyclopedia Britannica. https://www.britannica.com/event/Mukden-Incident

The Editors of Encyclopedia Britannica (2025, April 22). Nanjing Massacre. Encyclopedia Britannica. https://www.britannica.com/event/Nanjing-Massacre

The Editors of Encyclopedia Britannica (2025, April 5). Flying Tigers. Encyclopedia Britannica. https://www.britannica.com/topic/Flying-Tigers

Chan, H., Feuerwerker, A., Liu, J.T., Lewis, J.W., Wilbur, C.M., Young, E.P., Twitchett, D.C., Hsu, C., Chen, C., McKnight, B.E., White, L., Lieberthal, K.G., Zürcher, E., Keightley, D.N., Silbergeld, J., Rawski, E.S., Hucker, C.O., Suzuki, C., Franke, H., DeWoskin, K.J., Elman, B., Dull, J.L. (2025, May 19). China. Encyclopedia Britannica. https://www.britannica.com/place/China

The Editors of Encyclopedia Britannica (2025, February 11). Chinese Civil War. Encyclopedia Britannica. https://www.britannica.com/event/Chinese-Civil-War

The Editors of Encyclopedia Britannica (2025, January 7). Long March. Encyclopedia Britannica. https://www.britannica.com/event/Long-March

The Editors of Encyclopedia Britannica (2025, March 27). Great Leap Forward. Encyclopedia Britannica. https://www.britannica.com/event/Great-Leap-Forward

The Editors of Encyclopedia Britannica (2018, March 20). A Brief Overview of China's Cultural Revolution. Encyclopedia Britannica. https://www.britannica.com/story/chinas-cultural-revolution

Pletcher, K. (2025, April 25). one-child policy. Encyclopedia Britannica. https://www.britannica.com/topic/one-child-policy

The Editors of Encyclopedia Britannica (2025, April 20). Tiananmen Square incident. Encyclopedia Britannica. https://www.britannica.com/event/Tiananmen-Square-incident

Amundson, C.H., Brandt, A.R.V. (2025, March 12). aquaculture. Encyclopedia Britannica. https://www.britannica.com/topic/aquaculture

https://upload.wikimedia.org/wikipedia/commons/thumb/8/8e/Mina_padi_java_Pj_IMG-20150313-WA0004_%28cropped%29.jpg/660px-Mina_padi_java_Pj_IMG-20150313-WA0004_%28cropped%29.jpg

https://en.wikipedia.org/wiki/Rice-fish_system

https://www.travelchinaguide.com/intro/social_customs/zodiac/compatibility.htm?srsltid=AfmBOorJwkd8ncaVb8ciOtrRMDuYC1UfvgrzIPtbNk-WDEgQiHrAkiDLq

https://www.travelchinaguide.com/intro/chinese-zodiac-years-chart.htm?srsltid=AfmBOorSvznxGO11cV47D0TgrlpgjEadaJlEMYAf-2Gvl4Lkq55Et8unq

Comstock, F. (2025, March 28). Chinese zodiac. Encyclopedia Britannica. https://www.britannica.com/topic/Chinese-zodiac

https://cwp.missouri.edu/2014/the-legend-behind-zongzi/#:~:text=Zongzi%2C%20a%20traditional%20Chinese%20food,of%20Chu%20inWarring%20States%20Period

Murray, L. (2015, September 25). Shine On, Harvest Moon Festival. Encyclopedia Britannica. https://www.britannica.com/story/shine-on-harvest-moon-festival

Payne, Laura and Preston, Charles. "Dragon Boat Festival". Encyclopedia Britannica, 19 Dec. 2024, https://www.britannica.com/topic/Dragon-Boat-Festival

The Editors of Encyclopedia Britannica (2025, March 5). Chang'e. Encyclopedia Britannica. https://www.britannica.com/topic/Change-Chinese-deity

The Editors of Encyclopedia Britannica (2025, April 11). Atlantic City. Encyclopedia Britannica. https://www.britannica.com/place/Atlantic-City-New-Jersey

Cunningham, J.M. (2025, April 4). Miss America. Encyclopedia Britannica. https://www.britannica.com/topic/Miss-America-Pageant

Monaco, P. (2021, April 19). *Sonora Webster Carver: Fearless horse diving girl.* The Spectrum. https://www.thespectrum.com/story/sports/mesquite/2021/04/18/eighth-pole-sonora-webster-carver-fearless-horse-diving-girl/7281572002

Steel Piers Diving Horse, Lake County Museum, Curt Teich Collection. Postcard

Atlantic City, N.J. Miss America, Jack Freeman Inc. Postcard

www.ingramcontent.com/pod-product-compliance
Lightning Source LLC
Chambersburg PA
CBHW061746120626
46550CB00005B/1910